CASENOTE LEGAL BRIEFS

FEDERAL COURTS

Adaptable to courses utilizing Redish and Nichols' casebook on Federal Courts

NORMAN S. GOLDENBERG, SENIOR EDITOR
PETER TENEN, MANAGING EDITOR

STAFF WRITERS
DIANE FOLEY JONES
INGE VAN HERLE

PUBLISHED BY **CASENOTES PUBLISHING CO., INC. 1640 5th ST., SUITE 208 SANTA MONICA, CA 90401**

ISBN 0-87457-218-5

FORMAT OF THE CASENOTE LEGAL BRIEF

CASE CAPSULE: This bold-faced section (first three paragraphs) highlights the procedural nature of the case, a short summary of the facts, and the rule of law. This is an invaluable quick-review device designed to refresh the student's memory for classroom discussion and exam preparation.

NATURE OF CASE: This section identifies the form of action (e.g., breach of contract, negligence, battery), the type of proceeding (e.g., demurrer, appeal from trial court's jury instructions) and the relief sought (e.g., damages, injunction, criminal sanctions).

FACT SUMMARY: The fact summary is included to refresh the student's memory. It can be used as a quick reminder of the facts when the student is chosen by an instructor to brief a case.

CONCISE RULE OF LAW: This portion of the brief summarizes the general principle of law that the case illustrates. Like the fact summary, it is included to refresh the student's memory. It may be used for instant recall of the court's holding and for classroom discussion or home review.

FACTS: This section contains all relevant facts of the case, including the contentions of the parties and the lower court holdings. It is written in a logical order to give the student a clear understanding of the case. The plaintiff and defendant are identified by their proper names throughout and are always labeled with a (P) or (D).

ISSUE: The issue is a concise question that brings out the essence of the opinion as it relates to the section of the casebook in which the case appears. Both substantive and procedural issues are included if relevant to the decision.

HOLDING AND DECISION: This section offers a clear and in-depth discussion of the rule of the case and the court's rationale. It is written in easy-to-understand language. When relevant, it includes a thorough discussion of the exceptions listed by the court, the concurring and dissenting opinions, and the names of the judges.

CONCURRENCE / DISSENT: All concurrences and dissents are briefed whenever they are included by the casebook editor.

EDITOR'S ANALYSIS: This last paragraph gives the student a broad understanding of where the case "fits in" with other cases in the section of the book and with the entire course. It is a hornbook-style discussion indicating whether the case is a majority or minority opinion and comparing the principal case with other cases in the casebook. It may also provide analysis from restatements, uniform codes, and law review articles. The editor's analysis will prove to be invaluable to classroom discussion.

CROSS-REFERENCE TO OUTLINE: Wherever possible, following each case is a cross-reference linking the subject matter of the issue to the appropriate place in the *Casenote Law Outline,* which provides further information on the subject.

WINTER v. G.P. PUTNAM'S SONS

938 F.2d 1033 (1991).

NATURE OF CASE: Appeal from summary judgment in a products liability action.

FACT SUMMARY: Winter (P) relied on a book on mushrooms published by Putnam (D) and became critically ill after eating a poisonous mushroom.

CONCISE RULE OF LAW: Strict products liability is not applicable to the expressions contained within a book.

FACTS: Winter (P) purchased The Encyclopedia of Mushrooms, a book published by Putnam (D), to help in collecting and eating wild mushrooms. In 1988, Winter (P), relying on descriptions in the book, ate some wild mushrooms which turned out to be poisonous. Winter (P) became so ill he required a liver transplant. He brought a strict products liability action against Putnam (D), alleging that the book contained erroneous and misleading information that caused his injury. Putnam (D) responded that the information in the book was not a product for purposes of strict products liability, and the trial court granted its motion for summary judgment. The trial court also rejected Winter's (P) actions for negligence and misrepresentation. Winter (P) appealed.

ISSUE: Is strict products liability applicable to the expressions contained within a book?

HOLDING AND DECISION: (Sneed, J.) No. Strict products liability is not applicable to the expressions contained within a book. Products liability is geared toward tangible objects. The expression of ideas is governed by copyright, libel, and misrepresentation laws. The Restatement (Second) of Torts lists examples of the items that are covered by §402A strict liability. All are tangible items, such as tires or automobiles. There is no indication that the doctrine should be expanded beyond this area. Furthermore, there is a strong public interest in the unfettered exchange of ideas. The threat of liability without fault could seriously inhibit persons who wish to share thoughts and ideas with others. Although some courts have held that aeronautical charts are products for purposes of strict liability, these charts are highly technical tools which resemble compasses. The Encyclopedia of Mushrooms, published by Putnam (D), is a book of pure thought and expression and therefore does not constitute a product for purposes of strict liability. Additionally, publishers do not owe a duty to investigate the contents of books that they distribute. Therefore, a negligence action may not be maintained by Winter (P) against Putnam (D). Affirmed.

EDITOR'S ANALYSIS: This decision is in accord with the rulings in most jurisdictions. See Alm v. Nostrand Reinhold Co., Inc., 480 N.E. 2d 1263 (Ill. 1985). The court also stated that since the publisher is not a guarantor of the accuracy of an author's statements, an action for negligent misrepresentation could not be maintained. The elements of negligent misrepresentation are stated in § 311 of the Restatement (Second) of Torts.

[For more information on misrepresentation, see Casenote Law Outline on Torts, Chapter 12, § III, Negligent Misrepresentation.]

NOTE TO THE STUDENT

OUR GOAL. It is the goal of Casenotes Publishing Company, Inc. to create and distribute the finest, clearest and most accurate legal briefs available. To this end, we are constantly seeking new ideas, comments and constructive criticism. As a user of *Casenote Legal Briefs,* your suggestions will be highly valued. With all correspondence, please include your complete name, address, and telephone number, including area code and zip code.

THE TOTAL STUDY SYSTEM. Casenote Legal Briefs are just one part of the Casenotes TOTAL STUDY SYSTEM. Most briefs are (wherever possible) cross-referenced to the appropriate *Casenote Law Outline,* which will elaborate on the issue at hand. By purchasing a Law Outline together with your Legal Brief, you will have both parts of the Casenotes TOTAL STUDY SYSTEM. (See the advertising in the front of this book for a list of Law Outlines currently available.)

A NOTE ABOUT LANGUAGE. Please note that the language used in *Casenote Legal Briefs* in reference to minority groups and women reflects terminology used within the historical context of the time in which the respective courts wrote the opinions. We at Casenotes Publishing Co., Inc. are well aware of and very sensitive to the desires of all people to be treated with dignity and to be referred to as they prefer. Because such preferences change from time to time, and because the language of the courts reflects the time period in which opinions were written, our case briefs will not necessarily reflect contemporary references. We appreciate your understanding and invite your comments.

EDITOR'S NOTE. Casenote Legal Briefs are intended to supplement the student's casebook, not replace it. There is no substitute for the student's own mastery of this important learning and study technique. If used properly, *Casenote Legal Briefs* are an effective law study aid that will serve to reinforce the student's understanding of the cases.

REF. # 1364-96-696

SUPPLEMENT REQUEST FORM

At the time this book was printed, a brief was included for every major case in the casebook and for every existing supplement to the casebook. However, if a new supplement to the casebook (or a new edition of the casebook) has been published since this publication was printed and if that casebook supplement (or new edition of the casebook) was available for sale at the time you purchased this Casenote Legal Briefs book, we will be pleased to provide you the new cases contained therein AT NO CHARGE when you send us a stamped, self-addressed envelope.

TO OBTAIN YOUR FREE SUPPLEMENT MATERIAL, **YOU MUST FOLLOW THE INSTRUCTIONS BELOW PRECISELY** OR YOUR REQUEST WILL NOT BE ACKNOWLEDGED!

1. Please check if there is in fact an existing supplement and, if so, that the cases are not already included in your Casenote Legal Briefs. Check the main table of cases as well as the supplement table of cases, if any.
2. **REMOVE THIS ENTIRE PAGE FROM THE BOOK.** You MUST send this ORIGINAL page to receive your supplement. This page acts as your proof of purchase and contains the reference number necessary to fill your supplement request properly. No photocopy of this page or written request will be honored or answered. Any request from which the reference number has been removed, altered or obliterated will not be honored.
3. ✶ Prepare a STAMPED self-addressed envelope for return mailing. Be sure to use a FULL SIZE (9 X 12) ENVELOPE (MANILA TYPE) so that the supplement will fit and AFFIX ENOUGH POSTAGE TO COVER 3 OZ. **ANY SUPPLEMENT REQUEST NOT ACCOMPANIED BY A STAMPED SELF-ADDRESSED ENVELOPE WILL ABSOLUTELY NOT BE FILLED OR ACKNOWLEDGED.**
4. MULTIPLE SUPPLEMENT REQUESTS: If you are ordering more than one supplement, we suggest that you enclose a stamped, self-addressed envelope for each supplement requested. If you enclose only one envelope for a multiple request, your order may not be filled immediately should any supplement which you requested still be in production. In other words, your order will be held by us until it can be filled completely.
5. Casenotes prints two kinds of supplements. A "New Edition" supplement is issued when a new edition of your casebook is published. A "New Edition" supplement gives you all major cases found in the new edition of the casebook which did not appear in the previous edition. A regular "supplement" is issued when a paperback supplement to your casebook is published. If the box at the lower right is stamped, then the "New Edition" supplement was provided to your bookstore and is *not* available from Casenotes; however, Casenotes will still send you any regular "supplements" which have been printed either before or after the new edition of your casebook appeared and which, according to the reference number at the top of this page, have not been included in this book. If the box is not stamped, Casenotes will send you any supplements, "New Edition" and/or regular, needed to completely update your Casenote Legal Briefs.

✶☞ ***NOTE:* REQUESTS FOR SUPPLEMENTS WILL NOT BE FILLED UNLESS THESE INSTRUCTIONS ARE COMPLIED WITH!**

6. Fill in the following information:

Full title of CASEBOOK **FEDERAL COURTS**

CASEBOOK author's name **Redish and Nichols**

Date of new supplement you are requesting ______________

Name and location of bookstore where this Casenote Legal Brief was purchased ______________

Name and location of law school you attend ______________

Any comments regarding Casenote Legal Briefs ______________

NOTE: IF THIS BOX IS STAMPED, NO NEW EDITION SUPPLEMENT CAN BE OBTAINED BY MAIL.

PUBLISHED BY **CASENOTES PUBLISHING CO., INC. 1640 5th ST, SUITE 208 SANTA MONICA, CA 90401**

PLEASE PRINT

NAME ______________ **PHONE** ______________ **DATE** ______________

ADDRESS/CITY/STATE/ZIP ______________

LAW OUTLINES from CASENOTE™

the Ultimate Outline

- ***WRITTEN BY NATIONALLY RECOGNIZED AUTHORITIES IN THEIR FIELD.***
- ***FEATURING A FLEXIBLE, SUBJECT-ORIENTED APPROACH.***
- ***CONTAINS: TABLE OF CONTENTS; CAPSULE OUTLINE; FULL OUTLINE; EXAM PREPARATION; GLOSSARY; TABLE OF CASES; TABLE OF AUTHORITIES; CASEBOOK CROSS REFERENCE CHART; INDEX.***
- ***THE TOTAL LAW SUMMARY UTILIZING THE MOST COMPREHENSIVE STUDY APPROACH IN THE MOST EFFECTIVE, EASY-TO-READ FORMAT.***

REF #	SUBJECT	AUTHORS	RETAIL PRICE
#5260	**ADMINISTRATIVE LAW**	by **Charles H. Koch, Jr.,** Dudley W. Woodbridge Professor of Law, College of William and Mary. **Sidney A. Shapiro,** John M. Rounds Professor of Law, University of Kansas. (1994)	(effective 7/1/96) **$18.95**
#5040	**CIVIL PROCEDURE**	by **John B. Oakley,** Professor of Law, University of California, Davis. **Rex R. Perschbacher,** Professor of Law & Associate Dean, Academic Affairs, University of California, Davis. (1996)	**$19.95**
	COMMERCIAL LAW	(*see* **5700 SALES • 5710 SECURED TRANS. • 5720 NEG. INSTRUMENTS & PMT. SYST.**)	
#5070	**CONFLICT OF LAWS**	by **Luther L. McDougal, III,** W.R. Irby Professor of Law, Tulane University. **Robert L. Felix,** James P. Mozingo, III Prof. of Law, Univ. of S. Carolina. (1992)	**$18.95**
#5080	**CONSTITUTIONAL LAW**	by **Gary Goodpaster,** Prof. of Law, Univ. of California, Davis. (1994 w/'95 supp)	**$21.95**
#5010	**CONTRACTS**	by **Daniel Wm. Fessler,** Professor of Law, University of California, Davis. (1996)	**$18.95**
#5050	**CORPORATIONS** AND ALTERNATIVE BUSINESS VEHICLES	by **Lewis D. Solomon,** Arthur Selwin Miller Research Prof. of Law, George Washington Univ. **Daniel Wm. Fessler,** Prof. of Law, University of California, Davis. **Arthur E. Wilmarth, Jr.,** Assoc. Prof. of Law, George Washington University. (1994)	**$20.95**
#5020	**CRIMINAL LAW**	by **Joshua Dressler,** Professor of Law, McGeorge School of Law. (1996)	**$18.95**
#5200	**CRIMINAL PROCEDURE**	by **Joshua Dressler,** Prof. of Law, McGeorge School of Law. (1993 w/'95 supp.)	**$17.95**
#5800	**ESTATE & GIFT TAX** INCLUDING THE FEDERAL GENERATION-SKIPPING TAX	by **Joseph M. Dodge,** W.H. Francis Prof. of Law, University of Texas at Austin. (1993)	**$18.95**
#5060	**EVIDENCE**	by **Kenneth Graham, Jr.,** Professor of Law, University of California, Los Angeles. (1996)	**$19.95**
#5300	**FEDERAL COURTS**	by **Howard P. Fink,** Isadore and Ida Topper Prof. of Law, Ohio State University. **Linda S. Mullenix,** Bernard J. Ward Centennial Prof. of Law, Univ. of Texas. (1996)	**TBA**
#5210	**FEDERAL INCOME TAXATION**	by **Joseph M. Dodge,** W.H. Francis Professor of Law, University of Texas at Austin (1994).	**$19.95**
#5300	**LEGAL RESEARCH**	by **Nancy L. Schultz,** Assistant Dean and Dir., Research and Writing, George Washington Univ. Nat'l Law Center. **Louis J. Sirico, Jr.,** Professor of Law and Director of Legal Writing, Villanova University. (1996)	**$18.95**
#5720	**NEGOTIABLE INST. & PMT. SYST.**	by **Donald B. King,** Professor of Law, Saint Louis University **Peter Winship,** James Cleo Thompson, Sr. Trustee Prof., SMU. (1995)	**$18.95**
#5030	**PROPERTY**	by **Sheldon F. Kurtz,** Percy Bordwell Professor of Law, University of Iowa.	**TBA**
#5700	**SALES**	by **Robert E. Scott,** Dean and Lewis F. Powell, Jr. Professor of Law, University of Virginia. **Donald B. King,** Professor of Law, Saint Louis University. (1992 w/'96 supp.)	**$18.95**
#5710	**SECURED TRANSACTIONS**	by **Donald B. King,** Professor of Law, Saint Louis University. (1995 w/'96 supp.)	**$17.95**
#5000	**TORTS**	by **George C. Christie,** James B. Duke Professor of Law, Duke University. **Jerry J. Phillips,** W.P. Toms Professor of Law & Chair, Committee on Admissions, University of Tennessee. (1996)	**$19.95**
#5220	**WILLS, TRUSTS & ESTATES**	by **William M. McGovern,** Professor of Law, University of California, Los Angeles. (1996)	**$19.95**

casenote™ Legal Briefs

PRICE LIST — EFFECTIVE JULY 1, 1996 ● PRICES SUBJECT TO CHANGE WITHOUT NOTICE

Ref. No.	Course	Adaptable to Courses Utilizing	Retail Price
1265	ADMINISTRATIVE LAW	BONFIELD & ASIMOV	16.00
1263	ADMINISTRATIVE LAW	BREYER, STEWART & SUNSTEIN	18.00
1266	ADMINISTRATIVE LAW	CASS, DIVER & BEERMAN	16.00
1260	ADMINISTRATIVE LAW	GELLHORN, B., S., R., S. & F.	16.00
1264	ADMINISTRATIVE LAW	MASHAW, MERRILL & SHANE	17.50
1262	ADMINISTRATIVE LAW	SCHWARTZ	17.00
1290	ADMIRALTY	HEALY & SHARPE	20.00
1291	ADMIRALTY	LUCAS	17.50
1350	AGENCY & PARTNERSHIP (ENT.ORG)	CONARD, KNAUSS & SIEGEL	20.00
1351	AGENCY & PARTNERSHIP	HYNES	19.00
1281	ANTITRUST (TRADE REGULATION)	HANDLER, B. P. & G.	16.50
1283	ANTITRUST	SULLIVAN & HOVENKAMP	17.00
1611	BANKING LAW	MACEY & MILLER	16.00
1610	BANKING LAW	SYMONS & WHITE	14.00
1303	BANKRUPTCY (DEBTOR-CREDITOR)	EISENBERG	18.00
1440	BUSINESS PLANNING	HERWITZ	12.50
1040	CIVIL PROCEDURE	COUND, F., M. & S	19.00
1043	CIVIL PROCEDURE	FIELD, KAPLAN & CLERMONT	19.00
1041	CIVIL PROCEDURE	HAZARD, TAIT & FLETCHER	18.00
1047	CIVIL PROCEDURE	MARCUS, REDISH & SHERMAN	18.00
1044	CIVIL PROCEDURE	ROSENBERG, S. & D.	19.00
1046	CIVIL PROCEDURE	YEAZELL	16.00
1311	COMM'L LAW	FARNSWORTH, H., R., H. & M.	18.00
1312	COMM'L LAW	JORDAN & WARREN	18.00
1310	COMM'L LAW (SALES/SEC.TR./PAY.LAW [Sys.])	SPEIDEL, SUMMERS & WHITE	20.00
1313	COMM'L LAW (SALES/SEC.TR./PAY.LAW)	WHALEY	17.00
1320	COMMUNITY PROPERTY	BIRD	16.50
1630	COMPARATIVE LAW	SCHLESINGER, B., D., & H.	15.00
1048	COMPLEX LITIGATION	MARCUS & SHERMAN	16.00
1072	CONFLICTS	BRILMAYER	16.00
1071	CONFLICTS	CRAMTON, CURRIE & KAY	16.00
1070	CONFLICTS	ROSENBERG, HAY & WEINTRAUB	19.00
1086	CONSTITUTIONAL LAW	BREST & LEVINSON	17.00
1082	CONSTITUTIONAL LAW	COHEN & VARAT	20.00
1088	CONSTITUTIONAL LAW	FARBER, ESKRIDGE & FRICKEY	17.00
1080	CONSTITUTIONAL LAW	GUNTHER	18.00
1081	CONSTITUTIONAL LAW	LOCKHART, K., C., S. & F.	17.00
1085	CONSTITUTIONAL LAW	ROTUNDA	19.00
1087	CONSTITUTIONAL LAW	STONE, S., S. & T.	18.00
1017	CONTRACTS	CALAMARI, PERILLO & BENDER	22.00
1101	CONTRACTS	CRANDALL & WHALEY	19.00
1014	CONTRACTS	DAWSON, HARVEY & HENDRESON	18.00
1010	CONTRACTS	FARNSWORTH & YOUNG	17.00
1011	CONTRACTS	FULLER & EISENBERG	19.00
1100	CONTRACTS	HAMILTON, RAU & WEINTRAUB	18.00
1013	CONTRACTS	KESSLER, GILMORE & KRONMAN	22.00
1016	CONTRACTS	KNAPP & CRYSTAL	19.50
1012	CONTRACTS	MURPHY & SPEIDEL	21.00
1018	CONTRACTS	MURRAY	21.00
1015	CONTRACTS	ROSETT	20.00
1019	CONTRACTS	VERNON	19.00
1502	COPYRIGHT	GOLDSTEIN	17.00
1501	COPYRIGHT	NIMMER, M., M., & N.	18.50
1218	CORPORATE TAXATION	LIND, S. L. & R	13.00
1050	CORPORATIONS	CARY & EISENBERG (ABR. & UNABR.)	18.00
1054	CORPORATIONS	CHOPER, MORRIS & COFFEE	20.50
1350	CORPORATIONS (ENTERPRISE ORG.)	CONARD, KNAUSS & SIEGEL	20.00
1053	CORPORATIONS	HAMILTON	18.00
1057	CORPORATIONS	O'KELLEY & THOMPSON	17.00
1056	CORPORATIONS	SOLOMON, S., B., & W.	18.00
1052	CORPORATIONS	VAGTS	16.00
1300	CREDITOR'S RIGHTS (DEBTOR-CREDITOR)	RIESENFELD	20.00
1550	CRIMINAL JUSTICE	WEINREB	17.00
1020	CRIMINAL LAW	BOYCE & PERKINS	21.00
1024	CRIMINAL LAW	DIX & SHARLOT	16.00
1028	CRIMINAL LAW	DRESSLER	20.00
1027	CRIMINAL LAW	JOHNSON	19.00
1021	CRIMINAL LAW	KADISH & SCHULHOFER	18.00
1026	CRIMINAL LAW	KAPLAN, WEISBERG & BINDER	17.00
1023	CRIMINAL LAW	LAFAVE	18.00
1022	CRIMINAL LAW	WEINREB	14.00
1205	CRIMINAL PROCEDURE	ALLEN, KUHNS & STUNTZ	16.00
1202	CRIMINAL PROCEDURE	HADDAD, Z., S. & B.	19.00
1200	CRIMINAL PROCEDURE	KAMISAR, LAFAVE & ISRAEL	18.00
1204	CRIMINAL PROCEDURE	SALTZBURG & CAPRA	16.00
1203	CRIMINAL PROCEDURE (PROCESS)	WEINREB	17.50
1303	DEBTOR-CREDITOR	EISENBERG	18.00
1302	DEBTOR-CREDITOR	EPSTEIN, LANDERS & NICKLES	17.00
1300	DEBTOR-CREDITOR (CRED. RTS.)	RIESENFELD	20.00
1304	DEBTOR-CREDITOR	WARREN & WESTBROOK	18.00
1224	DECEDENTS ESTATES	RITCHIE, ALFORD, EFFLAND & DORIS	20.00
1222	DECEDENTS ESTATES	SCOLES & HALBACH	20.50
1231	DECEDENTS ESTATES (TRUSTS)	WAGGONER, WELLMAN, A. & F.	19.00
	DOMESTIC RELATIONS (*see* FAMILY LAW)		
3000	EDUCATION LAW (COURSE OUTLINE)	AQUILA & PETZKE	25.50
1670	EMPLOYMENT DISCRIMINATION	FRIEDMAN & STRICKLER	16.00
1671	EMPLOYMENT DISCRIMINATION	ZIMMER, SULLIVAN, R. & C.	17.00
1660	EMPLOYMENT LAW	ROTHSTEIN, KNAPP & LIEBMAN	18.50
1350	ENTERPRISE ORGANIZATION	CONARD, KNAUSS & SIEGEL	20.00
1342	ENVIRONMENTAL LAW	ANDERSON, MANDELKER & TARLOCK	15.00
1341	ENVIRONMENTAL LAW	FINDLEY & FARBER	17.00
1345	ENVIRONMENTAL LAW	MENELL & STEWART	16.00
1344	ENVIRONMENTAL LAW	PERCIVAL, MILLER, S. & L.	17.00
1343	ENVIRONMENTAL LAW	PLATER, ABRAMS & GOLDFARB	16.00
	EQUITY (*see* REMEDIES)		
1217	ESTATE & GIFT TAXATION	BITTKER, CLARK & McCOUCH	14.00
1214	ESTATE & GIFT TAXATION	KAHN & WAGGONER	16.00
1213	ESTATE & GIFT TAX (FED. WEALTH TRANS.)	SURREY, MCDANIEL & GUTMAN	15.00
	ETHICS (*see* PROFESSIONAL RESPONSIBILITY)		
1065	EVIDENCE	GREEN & NESSON	19.00
1063	EVIDENCE	LEMPERT & SALTZBURG	11.00
1066	EVIDENCE	MUELLER & KIRKPATRICK	16.00
1064	EVIDENCE	STRONG, BROUN & MOUSTELLER.	21.50
1062	EVIDENCE	SUTTON & WELLBORN	21.00
1061	EVIDENCE	WALTZ & PARK	19.00
1060	EVIDENCE	WEINSTEIN, M., A. & B.	21.50
1244	FAMILY LAW (DOMESTIC RELATION)	AREEN	21.00
1242	FAMILY LAW (DOMESTIC RELATION)	CLARK & GLOWINSKY	18.00
1245	FAMILY LAW (DOMESTIC RELATION)	ELLMAN, KURTZ & BARTLETT	19.00
1243	FAMILY LAW (DOMESTIC RELATION)	KRAUSE	23.00
1240	FAMILY LAW (DOMESTIC RELATION)	WADLINGTON	19.00
1231	FAMILY PROPERTY LAW (WILLS/TRUSTS)	WAGGONER, WELLMAN, A. & F.	19.00
1362	FEDERAL COURTS	CURRIE	16.00
1360	FEDERAL COURTS	FALLON, M. & S. (HART & WECHSLER)	18.00
1360	FEDERAL COURTS	HART & WECHSLER (FALLON et al)	18.00
1363	FEDERAL COURTS	LOW & JEFFRIES	15.00
1361	FEDERAL COURTS	McCORMICK, C. & W.	19.00
1364	FEDERAL COURTS	REDISH & NICHOL	16.00
1510	GRATUITOUS TRANSFERS	CLARK, LUSKY & MURPHY	17.00
1650	HEALTH LAW	FURROW, J., J., & S.	16.50
1640	IMMIGRATION LAW	ALEINIKOFF, MARTIN & MOTOMURA	15.00
1371	INSURANCE LAW	KEETON	20.00
1372	INSURANCE LAW	YORK, WHELAN & MARTINEZ	18.00
1370	INSURANCE LAW	YOUNG & HOLMES	16.00
1394	INTERNATIONAL BUSINESS TRANSACTIONS	FOLSOM, GORDON & SPANOGLE	14.00
1393	INTERNATIONAL LAW	CARTER & TRIMBLE	15.00
1392	INTERNATIONAL LAW	HENKIN, P., S. & S.	16.00
1390	INTERNATIONAL LAW	OLIVER, F., B., S., & W.	21.00
1331	LABOR LAW	COX, BOK, GORMAN & FINKIN	18.00
1332	LABOR LAW	HARPER & ESTREICHER	19.00
1333	LABOR LAW	LESLIE	17.50
1330	LABOR LAW	MERRIFIELD, S. & C.	18.00
1471	LAND FINANCE (REAL ESTATE TRANS)	BERGER & JOHNSTONE	17.00
1620	LAND FINANCE (REAL ESTATE TRANS)	NELSON & WHITMAN	18.00
1470	LAND FINANCE	PENNEY, B. & C.	15.00
1452	LAND USE	CALLIES, FREILICH & ROBERTS	16.00
1450	LAND USE	WRIGHT & GITELMAN	22.00
1421	LEGISLATION	ESKRIDGE & FRICKEY	14.00
1590	LOCAL GOVERNMENT LAW	VALENTE & McCARTHY	21.00
1480	MASS MEDIA	FRANKLIN & ANDERSON	14.00
1312	NEGOTIABLE INSTRUMENTS (COMM. LAW)	JORDAN & WARREN	18.00
1313	NEGOTIABLE INSTRUMENTS (COMM. LAW)	WHALEY	17.00
1570	NEW YORK PRACTICE	PETERFREUND & McLAUGHLIN	24.00
1541	OIL & GAS	KUNTZ, L., A. & S.	17.00
1540	OIL & GAS	MAXWELL, WILLIAMS, M. & K.	17.00
1560	PATENT LAW	FRANCIS & COLLINS (CHOATE)	22.00
1310	PAYMENT LAW [SYST.][COMM. LAW]	SPEIDEL, SUMMERS & WHITE	20.00
1313	PAYMENT LAW (COMM.LAW / NEG. INST.)	WHALEY	17.00
1431	PRODUCTS LIABILITY	OWEN, MONTGOMERY & KEETON	19.00
1091	PROF. RESPONSIBILITY (ETHICS)	GILLERS	12.00
1093	PROF. RESPONSIBILITY (ETHICS)	HAZARD, KONIAK, & CRAMTON	17.00
1092	PROF. RESPONSIBILITY (ETHICS)	MORGAN & ROTUNDA	12.00
1030	PROPERTY	CASNER & LEACH	20.00
1031	PROPERTY	CRIBBET, JOHNSON, FINLEY & SMITH	20.50
1037	PROPERTY	DONAHUE, KAUPER & MARTIN	17.00
1035	PROPERTY	DUKEMINIER & KRIER	17.00
1034	PROPERTY	HAAR & LIEBMAN	19.50
1036	PROPERTY	KURTZ & HOVENKAMP	18.00
1033	PROPERTY	NELSON, STOEBUCK, & WHITMAN.	19.50
1032	PROPERTY	RABIN & KWALL	19.00
1038	PROPERTY	SINGER	17.50
1621	REAL ESTATE TRANSACTIONS	GOLDSTEIN & KORNGOLD	17.00
1471	REAL ESTATE TRANS. & FIN. (LAND FINANCE)	BERGER & JOHNSTONE	16.00
1620	REAL ESTATE TRANSFER & FINANCE	NELSON & WHITMAN	17.00
1254	REMEDIES (EQUITY)	LAYCOCK	19.00
1253	REMEDIES (EQUITY)	LEAVELL, L., N. & K/F.	20.00
1252	REMEDIES (EQUITY)	RE & RE	22.00
1255	REMEDIES (EQUITY)	SHOBEN & TABB	21.50
1250	REMEDIES (EQUITY)	YORK, BAUMAN & RENDLEMAN	24.00
1312	SALES (COMM. LAW)	JORDAN & WARREN	18.00
1310	SALES (COMM. LAW)	SPEIDEL, SUMMERS & WHITE	20.00
1313	SALES (COMM. LAW)	WHALEY	17.00
1312	SECURED TRANS. (COMM. LAW)	JORDAN & WARREN	18.00
1310	SECURED TRANS.	SPEIDEL, SUMMERS & WHITE	20.00
1313	SECURED TRANS. (COMM. LAW)	WHALEY	17.00
1272	SECURITIES REGULATION	COX, HILLMAN, LANGEVOORT	17.00
1270	SECURITIES REGULATION	JENNINGS, MARSH & COFFEE	17.00
1271	SECURITIES REGULATION	RATNER	17.00
1680	SPORTS LAW	WEILER & ROBERTS	16.50
1215	TAXATION (BASIC FED. INC.)	ANDREWS	20.00
1217	TAXATION (ESTATE & GIFT)	BITTKER, CLARK & McCOUCH	14.00
1212	TAXATION (FED. INC.)	FREELAND, LIND & STEPHENS	17.00
1211	TAXATION (FED. INC.)	GRAETZ & SCHENK	16.00
1214	TAXATION (ESTATE & GIFT)	KAHN & WAGGONER	16.00
1210	TAXATION (FED. INC.)	KLEIN & BANKMAN	17.00
1218	TAXATION (CORPORATE)	LIND, S., L. & R.	13.00
1213	TAXATION (FED. WEALTH TRANS.)	SURREY, MCDANIEL & GUTMAN.	15.00
1006	TORTS	DOBBS	18.00
1003	TORTS	EPSTEIN	19.50
1004	TORTS	FRANKLIN & RABIN	16.50
1001	TORTS	HENDERSON, P. & S.	19.50
1002	TORTS	KEETON, K., S. & S.	22.00
1000	TORTS	PROSSER, W., S., K., & P.	23.00
1005	TORTS	SHULMAN, JAMES & GRAY	21.00
1281	TRADE REGULATION (ANTITRUST)	HANDLER, B., P. & G.	16.50
1230	TRUSTS	BOGERT, O., H., & H.	19.50
1231	TRUSTS/WILLS (FAMILY PROPERTY LAW)	WAGGONER, WELLMAN A. & F.	19.00
1410	U.C.C	EPSTEIN, MARTIN, H. & N.	14.00
1580	WATER LAW	TRELEASE & GOULD	18.00
1223	WILLS, TRUSTS & ESTATES	DUKEMINIER & JOHANSON	18.00
1220	WILLS	MECHEM & ATKINSON	19.00
1231	WILLS/TRUSTS (FAMILY PROPERTY LAW)	WAGGONER, WELLMAN A. & F.	19.00

(SERIES XXXIX)

CASENOTES PUBLISHING CO. INC. ● 1640 FIFTH STREET, SUITE 208 ● SANTA MONICA, CA 90401 ● (310) 395-6500

E-Mail Address- casenote@westworld.com

Website-http://www.casenotes.com

PLEASE PURCHASE FROM YOUR LOCAL BOOKSTORE. IF UNAVAILABLE, YOU MAY ORDER DIRECT.*

4TH CLASS POSTAGE (ALLOW TWO WEEKS) $1.00 PER ORDER; 1ST CLASS POSTAGE $3.00 (ONE BOOK), $2.00 EACH (TWO OR MORE BOOKS)

*CALIF. RESIDENTS PLEASE ADD 8¼% SALES TAX

NOTES

A GLOSSARY OF COMMON LATIN WORDS AND PHRASES ENCOUNTERED IN THE LAW

A FORTIORI: Because one fact exists or has been proven, therefore a second fact that is related to the first fact must also exist.

A PRIORI: From the cause to the effect. A term of logic used to denote that when one generally accepted truth is shown to be a cause, another particular effect must necessarily follow.

AB INITIO: From the beginning; a condition which has existed throughout, as in a marriage which was void ab initio.

ACTUS REUS: The wrongful act; in criminal law, such action sufficient to trigger criminal liability.

AD VALOREM: According to value; an ad valorem tax is imposed upon an item located within the taxing jurisdiction calculated by the value of such item.

AMICUS CURIAE: Friend of the court. Its most common usage takes the form of an amicus curiae brief, filed by a person who is not a party to an action but is nonetheless allowed to offer an argument supporting his legal interests.

ARGUENDO: In arguing. A statement, possibly hypothetical, made for the purpose of argument, is one made arguendo.

BILL QUIA TIMET: A bill to quiet title (establish ownership) to real property.

BONA FIDE: True, honest, or genuine. May refer to a person's legal position based on good faith or lacking notice of fraud (such as a bona fide purchaser for value) or to the authenticity of a particular document (such as a bona fide last will and testament).

CAUSA MORTIS: With approaching death in mind. A gift causa mortis is a gift given by a party who feels certain that death is imminent.

CAVEAT EMPTOR: Let the buyer beware. This maxim is reflected in the rule of law that a buyer purchases at his own risk because it is his responsibility to examine, judge, test, and otherwise inspect what he is buying.

CERTIORARI: A writ of review. Petitions for review of a case by the United States Supreme Court are most often done by means of a writ of certiorari.

CONTRA: On the other hand. Opposite. Contrary to.

CORAM NOBIS: Before us; writs of error directed to the court that originally rendered the judgment.

CORAM VOBIS: Before you; writs of error directed by an appellate court to a lower court to correct a factual error.

CORPUS DELICTI: The body of the crime; the requisite elements of a crime amounting to objective proof that a crime has been committed.

CUM TESTAMENTO ANNEXO, ADMINISTRATOR (ADMINISTRATOR C.T.A.): With will annexed; an administrator c.t.a. settles an estate pursuant to a will in which he is not appointed.

DE BONIS NON, ADMINISTRATOR (ADMINISTRATOR D.B.N.): Of goods not administered; an administrator d.b.n. settles a partially settled estate.

DE FACTO: In fact; in reality; actually. Existing in fact but not officially approved or engendered.

DE JURE: By right; lawful. Describes a condition that is legitimate "as a matter of law," in contrast to the term "de facto," which connotes something existing in fact but not legally sanctioned or authorized. For example, de facto segregation refers to segregation brought about by housing patterns, etc., whereas de jure segregation refers to segregation created by law.

DE MINIMUS: Of minimal importance; insignificant; a trifle; not worth bothering about.

DE NOVO: Anew; a second time; afresh. A trial de novo is a new trial held at the appellate level as if the case originated there and the trial at a lower level had not taken place.

DICTA: Generally used as an abbreviated form of obiter dicta, a term describing those portions of a judicial opinion incidental or not necessary to resolution of the specific question before the court. Such nonessential statements and remarks are not considered to be binding precedent.

DUCES TECUM: Refers to a particular type of writ or subpoena requesting a party or organization to produce certain documents in their possession.

EN BANC: Full bench. Where a court sits with all justices present rather than the usual quorum.

EX PARTE: For one side or one party only. An ex parte proceeding is one undertaken for the benefit of only one party, without notice to, or an appearance by, an adverse party.

EX POST FACTO: After the fact. An ex post facto law is a law that retroactively changes the consequences of a prior act.

EX REL.: Abbreviated form of the term ex relatione, meaning, upon relation or information. When the state brings an action in which it has no interest against an individual at the instigation of one who has a private interest in the matter.

FORUM NON CONVENIENS: Inconvenient forum. Although a court may have jurisdiction over the case, the action should be tried in a more conveniently located court, one to which parties and witnesses may more easily travel, for example.

GUARDIAN AD LITEM: A guardian of an infant as to litigation, appointed to represent the infant and pursue his/her rights.

HABEAS CORPUS: You have the body. The modern writ of habeas corpus is a writ directing that a person (body) being detained (such as a prisoner) be brought before the court so that the legality of his detention can be judicially ascertained.

IN CAMERA: In private, in chambers. When a hearing is held before a judge in his chambers or when all spectators are excluded from the courtroom.

IN FORMA PAUPERIS: In the manner of a pauper. A party who proceeds in forma pauperis because of his poverty is one who is allowed to bring suit without liability for costs.

INFRA: Below, under. A word referring the reader to a later part of a book. (The opposite of supra.)

IN LOCO PARENTIS: In the place of a parent.

IN PARI DELICTO: Equally wrong; a court of equity will not grant requested relief to an applicant who is in pari delicto, or as much at fault in the transactions giving rise to the controversy as is the opponent of the applicant.

IN PARI MATERIA: On like subject matter or upon the same matter. Statutes relating to the same person or things are said to be in pari materia. It is a general rule of statutory construction that such statutes should be construed together, i.e., looked at as if they together constituted one law.

IN PERSONAM: Against the person. Jurisdiction over the person of an individual.

IN RE: In the matter of. Used to designate a proceeding involving an estate or other property.

IN REM: A term that signifies an action against the res, or thing. An action in rem is basically one that is taken directly against property, as distinguished from an action in personam, i.e., against the person.

INTER ALIA: Among other things. Used to show that the whole of a statement, pleading, list, statute, etc., has not been set forth in its entirety.

INTER PARTES: Between the parties. May refer to contracts, conveyances or other transactions having legal significance.

INTER VIVOS: Between the living. An inter vivos gift is a gift made by a living grantor, as distinguished from bequests contained in a will, which pass upon the death of the testator.

IPSO FACTO: By the mere fact itself.

JUS: Law or the entire body of law.

LEX LOCI: The law of the place; the notion that the rights of parties to a legal proceeding are governed by the law of the place where those rights arose.

MALUM IN SE: Evil or wrong in and of itself; inherently wrong. This term describes an act that is wrong by its very nature, as opposed to one which would not be wrong but for the fact that there is a specific legal prohibition against it (malum prohibitum).

MALUM PROHIBITUM: Wrong because prohibited, but not inherently evil. Used to describe something that is wrong because it is expressly forbidden by law but that is not in and of itself evil, e.g., speeding.

MANDAMUS: We command. A writ directing an official to take a certain action.

MENS REA: A guilty mind; a criminal intent. A term used to signify the mental state that accompanies a crime or other prohibited act. Some crimes require only a general mens rea (general intent to do the prohibited act), but others, like assault with intent to murder, require the existence of a specific mens rea.

MODUS OPERANDI: Method of operating; generally refers to the manner or style of a criminal in committing crimes, admissible in appropriate cases as evidence of the identity of a defendant.

NEXUS: A connection to.

NISI PRIUS: A court of first impression. A nisi prius court is one where issues of fact are tried before a judge or jury.

N.O.V. (NON OBSTANTE VEREDICTO): Notwithstanding the verdict. A judgment n.o.v. is a judgment given in favor of one party despite the fact that a verdict was returned in favor of the other party, the justification being that the verdict either had no reasonable support in fact or was contrary to law.

NUNC PRO TUNC: Now for then. This phrase refers to actions that may be taken and will then have full retroactive effect.

PENDENTE LITE: Pending the suit; pending litigation underway.

PER CAPITA: By head; beneficiaries of an estate, if they take in equal shares, take per capita.

PER CURIAM: By the court; signifies an opinion ostensibly written "by the whole court" and with no identified author.

PER SE: By itself, in itself; inherently.

PER STIRPES: By representation. Used primarily in the law of wills to describe the method of distribution where a person, generally because of death, is unable to take that which is left to him by the will of another, and therefore his heirs divide such property between them rather than take under the will individually.

PRIMA FACIE: On its face, at first sight. A prima facie case is one that is sufficient on its face, meaning that the evidence supporting it is adequate to establish the case until contradicted or overcome by other evidence.

PRO TANTO: For so much; as far as it goes. Often used in eminent domain cases when a property owner receives partial payment for his land without prejudice to his right to bring suit for the full amount he claims his land to be worth.

QUANTUM MERUIT: As much as he deserves. Refers to recovery based on the doctrine of unjust enrichment in those cases in which a party has rendered valuable services or furnished materials that were accepted and enjoyed by another under circumstances that would reasonably notify the recipient that the rendering party expected to be paid. In essence, the law implies a contract to pay the reasonable value of the services or materials furnished.

QUASI: Almost like; as if; nearly. This term is essentially used to signify that one subject or thing is almost analogous to another but that material differences between them do exist. For example, a quasi-criminal proceeding is one that is not strictly criminal but shares enough of the same characteristics to require some of the same safeguards (e.g., procedural due process must be followed in a parol hearing).

QUID PRO QUO: Something for something. In contract law, the consideration, something of value, passed between the parties to render the contract binding.

RES GESTAE: Things done; in evidence law, this principle justifies the admission of a statement that would otherwise be hearsay when it is made so closely to the event in question as to be said to be a part of it, or with such spontaneity as not to have the possibility of falsehood.

RES IPSA LOQUITUR: The thing speaks for itself. This doctrine gives rise to a rebuttable presumption of negligence when the instrumentality causing the injury was within the exclusive control of the defendant, and the injury was one that does not normally occur unless a person has been negligent.

RES JUDICATA: A matter adjudged. Doctrine which provides that once a court of competent jurisdiction has rendered a final judgment or decree on the merits, that judgment or decree is conclusive upon the parties to the case and prevents them from engaging in any other litigation on the points and issues determined therein.

RESPONDEAT SUPERIOR: Let the master reply. This doctrine holds the master liable for the wrongful acts of his servant (or the principal for his agent) in those cases in which the servant (or agent) was acting within the scope of his authority at the time of the injury.

STARE DECISIS: To stand by or adhere to that which has been decided. The common law doctrine of stare decisis attempts to give security and certainty to the law by following the policy that once a principle of law as applicable to a certain set of facts has been set forth in a decision, it forms a precedent which will subsequently be followed, even though a different decision might be made were it the first time the question had arisen. Of course, stare decisis is not an inviolable principle and is departed from in instances where there is good cause (e.g., considerations of public policy led the Supreme Court to disregard prior decisions sanctioning segregation).

SUPRA: Above. A word referring a reader to an earlier part of a book.

ULTRA VIRES: Beyond the power. This phrase is most commonly used to refer to actions taken by a corporation that are beyond the power or legal authority of the corporation.

ADDENDUM OF FRENCH DERIVATIVES

IN PAIS: Not pursuant to legal proceedings.

CHATTEL: Tangible personal property.

CY PRES: Doctrine permitting courts to apply trust funds to purposes not expressed in the trust but necessary to carry out the settlor's intent.

PER AUTRE VIE: For another's life; in property law, an estate may be granted that will terminate upon the death of someone other than the grantee.

PROFIT A PRENDRE: A license to remove minerals or other produce from land.

VOIR DIRE: Process of questioning jurors as to their predispositions about the case or parties to a proceeding in order to identify those jurors displaying bias or prejudice.

TABLE OF CASES

NOTES

TABLE OF CASES (Continued)

CHAPTER 1
ISSUES IN JUDICIAL REVIEW

QUICK REFERENCE RULES OF LAW

1. **Duty of the Judicial Department.** The government of the United States is a government of laws and not of men, and it is the province and duty of the judicial department to say what the law is. (Marbury v. Madison)

2. **Standing.** In order to obtain standing, a plaintiff must show that the challenged action has caused him injury in fact, economic or otherwise. (Association of Data Processing Service Organizations, Inc. v. Camp)

3. **Exclusionary Zoning Practices.** A plaintiff who seeks to challenge exclusionary zoning practices must allege specific, concrete facts demonstrating that the challenged practices harm him and that he personally would benefit from the court's intervention. (Warth v. Seldin)

4. **Separation of Powers.** Under Article III of the U.S. Constitution, the principle of separation of powers counsels against recognizing standing in a case brought not to enforce specific obligations whose violation works a direct harm, but to seek a restructuring of the apparatus established by the Executive Branch to fulfill its legal duties. (Allen v. Wright)

5. **Standing.** Assertion of a right to a particular kind of government conduct, which the government has violated by acting differently, is insufficient to confer standing. (Valley Forge Christian College v. Americans United for Separation of Church and State)

6. **Mootness.** A case is moot if the controversy between the parties has clearly ceased to be definite and concrete and no longer touches the legal relations of parties having adverse legal interests. (DeFunis v. Odegaard)

7. **Ripeness.** The question of ripeness turns on the fitness of the issues for judicial decision and the hardship to the parties of withholding court consideration. (Pacific Gas & Electric Co. v. State Energy Resources Conservation & Development Commission)

8. **Nonjusticiable Controversy.** A controversy is nonjusticiable where there is a textually demonstrable constitutional commitment of the issue to a coordinate political department or a lack of judicially discoverable and manageable ways of resolving it. (Baker v. Carr)

9. **Impeachment.** The Senate has the sole authority to determine procedures for trying an impeached official, and such procedures are unreviewable by the courts. (Nixon v. United States)

1

NOTES

MARBURY v. MADISON

5 U.S. (1 Cranch) 137 (1803).

NATURE OF CASE: Action to enforce appointment of a commission to office.

FACT SUMMARY: Marbury (P) brought suit against Madison (D), the Secretary of State of the United States, after Marbury (P) had been appointed to a justice of the peace commission by then President Adams but which Madison (D), an appointee of the current President Jefferson, would not deliver to Marbury (P).

CONCISE RULE OF LAW: The government of the United States is a government of laws and not of men, and it is the province and duty of the judicial department to say what the law is.

FACTS: Marbury (P) brought suit against Madison (D), the Secretary of State of the United States, after Marbury (P) had been appointed to a justice of the peace commission by then President Adams but which Madison (D), an appointee of the current President Jefferson, would not deliver to Marbury (P). Marbury (P) demanded that Madison (D) show cause why a mandamus should not issue directing Madison (D) to deliver to Marbury (P) his commission. The U.S. Supreme Court then considered whether mandamus should issue.

ISSUE: Is the government of the United States a government of laws and not of men, and is it the province and duty of the judicial department to say what the law is?

HOLDING AND DECISION: (Marshall, C.J.) Yes. The government of the United States is a government of laws and not of men, and it is the province and duty of the judicial department to say what the law is. Here, the act to establish the judicial courts of the United States authorizes the Supreme Court to issue writs of mandamus in cases warranted by the principles and usages of law, to any courts appointed, or persons holding office, under the authority of the United States. The Secretary of State, being a person holding an office under the authority of the United States, is precisely within the letter of this description, and if this Court is not authorized to issue a writ of mandamus to such an officer, it must be because the law is unconstitutional and therefore absolutely incapable of conferring the authority and assigning the duties which its words purport to confer and assign. The U.S. Constitution has declared that the Supreme Court has original jurisdiction in all cases affecting ambassadors, other public ministers and consuls, and these in which a state shall be a party. In all other cases, the Supreme Court shall have appellate jurisdiction. To enable this court to issue a mandamus, it must be shown to be an exercise of appellate jurisdiction or to be necessary to enable them to exercise appellate jurisdiction. It is the essential criterion of appellate jurisdiction that it revises and corrects the proceedings in a cause already instituted and does not create that cause. Although, therefore, a mandamus may be directed to courts, yet to issue such a writ to an officer for the delivery of a paper is in effect to sustain an original action for that paper and thus does not seem to belong to appellate but to original jurisdiction. The authority, therefore, given to the Supreme Court by the act establishing the judicial courts of the United States to issue writs of mandamus to public officers appears not to be warranted by the Constitution. A legislative act, such as that establishing the judiciary, contrary to the Constitution is not law and cannot bind the courts and oblige them to give it effect. Thus, because a mandamus cannot issue from this Court unless it is an exercise of appellate jurisdiction and the mandamus demanded here appears to belong to original jurisdiction, the action must be dismissed.

EDITOR'S ANALYSIS: At its narrowest, the Marbury decision could be limited to the kind of defensive use of judicial review presented by its facts. A second, broader reading of the case stands for the proposition that it is the responsibility of the Supreme Court to apply the Constitution as the "supreme law of the land" to all cases properly presented for decision. Under the broadest interpretation of Marbury, it is the responsibility of courts, and, ultimately, the Supreme Court, to provide authoritative interpretations of the Constitution and to ensure enforcement of constitutional values.

NOTES:

WARTH v. SELDIN

422 U.S. 490 (1975).

NATURE OF CASE: Appeal from dismissal of complaint seeking to declare a zoning ordinance unconstitutional, an injunction against its enforcement, and actual and exemplary damages.

FACT SUMMARY: Warth (P) and other residents (P) of Rochester filed suit against the nearby town of Penfield (D), claiming that Penfield's (D) zoning ordinance excluded persons of low and moderate income from living in the town, thereby driving up Rochester's property taxes.

CONCISE RULE OF LAW: A plaintiff who seeks to challenge exclusionary zoning practices must allege specific, concrete facts demonstrating that the challenged practices harm him and that he personally would benefit from the court's intervention.

FACTS: Warth (P) resided in Rochester, which is located next to the Town of Penfield (D). Warth (P) and other Rochester residents (P) challenged Penfield's (D) zoning ordinance as unconstitutional, claiming that it excluded persons of low and moderate income, many of whom were members of racial or ethnic minorities. Penfield's (D) exclusionary practices in turn forced the city of Rochester to impose higher taxes on Warth (P) et al. in order to pay for its increased share of low-income housing. The district court dismissed the complaint for lack of standing, and the appellate court affirmed. The Supreme Court granted certiorari.

ISSUE: Must a plaintiff who seeks to challenge exclusionary zoning practices allege specific, concrete facts demonstrating that the challenged practices harm him and that he personally would benefit from the court's intervention?

HOLDING AND DECISION: (Powell, J.) Yes. A plaintiff who seeks to challenge exclusionary zoning practices must allege specific, concrete facts demonstrating that the challenged practices harm him and that he personally would benefit from the court's intervention. In this case, those plaintiffs who desire to live in Penfield (D) have not shown that, absent Penfield's (D) restrictive zoning practices, there was a substantial probability that they would actually have been able to purchase or lease homes in Penfield (D). In fact, there does not appear to be any actionable causal relationship between Penfield's (D) zoning practices and the asserted injury to those plaintiffs. The same is true for the second group of plaintiffs who assert standing on the basis of their status as taxpayers in Rochester. Moreover, these taxpayer-plaintiffs have not asserted any personal right under the Constitution or any statute to be free of actions by a neighboring city that have some adverse effect on Rochester. Affirmed.

DISSENT: (Brennan, J.) The majority denies standing to those plaintiffs who desire to live in Penfield (D) on the grounds that they cannot show that low-income projects would have satisfied their needs. But they should not be required to prove their case on paper in order to get into court.

EDITOR'S ANALYSIS: The prudential standing rule bars litigants from asserting the rights or legal interests of others in order to obtain relief for themselves. This rule of judicial self-governance is subject to several exceptions, however. Congress may remove it by statute, and it does not apply to First Amendment overbreadth challenges or when the person whose rights are being asserted cannot advance his own rights.

ASSOCIATION OF DATA PROCESSING SERVICE ORGANIZATIONS, INC. v. CAMP

397 U.S. 150 (1970).

NATURE OF CASE: Appeal from dismissal of challenge to an agency ruling.

FACT SUMMARY: Association of Data Processing Service Organizations (P) argued that, as a competitor of national banks engaged in data processing services, it had standing to challenge a Comptroller (D) ruling allowing such competition.

CONCISE RULE OF LAW: In order to obtain standing, a plaintiff must show that the challenged action has caused him injury in fact, economic or otherwise.

FACTS: The Comptroller of the Currency (D) issued a ruling permitting banks to offer data processing services to their customers. The Association (P), which sold data processing services and therefore stood to lose business due to the ruling, brought suit against the Comptroller (D) for violation of the Bank Service Corporation Act. The district court dismissed the complaint for lack of standing. The appeals court affirmed, stating that the Association (P) could not sue under the Act unless the Act gave it a "legal interest," that is, one of property, contract, or tort that would create an actionable right. The Association (P) appealed to the Supreme Court.

ISSUE: In order to obtain standing, must a plaintiff show that the challenged action has caused him injury in fact, economic or otherwise?

HOLDING AND DECISION: (Douglas, J.) Yes. In order to obtain standing, a plaintiff must show that the challenged action has caused him injury in fact, economic or otherwise. A plaintiff need not demonstrate the abrogation of a "legal interest." The "legal interest" test goes to the merits of a case. However, the interest sought to be protected — whether aesthetic, conservational, recreation, or economic — must be within the zone of interests to be protected by the statute in question. In this case, the Association (P), as a competitor of national banks that are engaging in data processing services, is within the class of persons aggrieved by the Comptroller's (D) action and, as such, is entitled to judicial review of the Comptroller's (D) ruling. Reversed.

EDITOR'S ANALYSIS: The injury-in-fact analysis first articulated by Justice Douglas is now the standard mode of inquiry in Article III standing determinations. Justice Douglas envisioned a broad definition of injury that would enlarge the class of people who could protest administrative action. This view has recently been compromised by recent Supreme Court decisions taking a narrower view of standing, at least as far as citizen environmental suits are concerned. See, for example, Lujan v. National Wildlife Federation, 497 U.S. 871 (1990) (plaintiffs must show actual use of the specific property in question in order to establish standing for injury to natural resources).

ALLEN v. WRIGHT

468 U.S. 737 (1984).

NATURE OF CASE: Appeal from grant of standing in class-action suit.

FACT SUMMARY: In Allen's (P) class-action suit against Wright (D) and the IRS (D) for the IRS's (D) failure to adopt sufficient standards to fulfill its obligation to deny tax-exempt status to racially discriminating private schools, Wright (D) contended that Allen (P) lacked standing to sue, and that the relief Allen (P) requested was contrary to the will of Congress expressed In a 1979 ban on strengthening IRS (D) guidelines.

CONCISE RULE OF LAW: Under Article III of the U.S. Constitution, the principle of separation of powers counsels against recognizing standing in a case brought not to enforce specific obligations whose violation works a direct harm, but to seek a restructuring of the apparatus established by the Executive Branch to fulfill its legal duties.

FACTS: Parents of black children, including Allen (P), brought a nationwide class-action suit against Wright (D) and the IRS (D), alleging that the IRS did not adopt sufficient standards and procedures to fulfill Its obligation to deny tax-exempt status to racially discriminatory private schools. Allen (P) asserted that the IRS (D) thereby harmed the class directly and interfered with the ability of their children to receive an education in desegregated private schools. The IRS (D) and Wright (D) contended that Allen (P) lacked standing to sue, that the judicial task proposed by Allen (P) was inappropriately intrusive for a federal court, and that the relief requested by Allen (P) would be contrary to the will of Congress expressed In a 1979 ban on strengthening IRS (D) guidelines. The district court granted Wright's motion to dismiss (D) Allen's (P) complaint on the ground that Allen lacked standing and that the relief requested by Allen (P) could be fashioned without large-scale judicial intervention in the administrative process. That court remanded the case to the district court. Certiorari was then granted by the U.S. Supreme Court.

ISSUE: Under Article III of the U.S. Constitution, does the principle of separation of powers counsel against recognizing standing in a case brought not to enforce a restructuring of the apparatus established by the Executive Branch to fulfill its legal duties.?

HOLDING AND DECISION: (O'Connor, J.) Yes. Under Article III of the U.S. Constitution, the principle of separation of powers counsels against recognizing standing in a case brought not to enforce specific legal obligations whose violation works a direct harm, but to seek a restructuring of the apparatus established by the Executive Branch to fulfill its legal duties. Allen (P) here alleged two injuries in his complaint to support class standing to bring this lawsuit. First, he stated that he was harmed directly by the mere fact of government financial aid to discriminatory private schools. Second, Allen (P) contended that the federal tax exemptions to racially discriminatory private schools in their communities impaired their ability to have their public schools desegregated. This Court concludes that neither alleged injury suffices to support Allen's (P) standing. The first fails under clear precedents of this Court because it does not constitute judicially cognizable injury. The second fails because the alleged injury is not fairly traceable to assertedly unlawful conduct of the IRS (D). The necessity that a plaintiff who seeks to invoke judicial power stand to profit in some personal interest remains an Article III requirement. Allen (P) has not met this fundamental requirement. Reversed.

DISSENT: (Brennan, J.) Here, Allen (P) has alleged at least one type of injury that satisfies the constitutional requirement of distinct and palpable injury. In particular, he has claimed that the IRS's (D) grant of tax-exempt status to racially discriminatory private schools directly injures the class's children's opportunity and ability to receive a desegregated education. It has been consistently recognized throughout the last thirty years that the deprivation of a child's right to receive an education in a desegregated school is a harm of special significance; surely it satisfies any constitutional requirement of injury in fact.

DISSENT: (Stevens, J.) Three propositions are clear here. (1) Allen (P) adequately alleged "injury in fact"; (2) the injury alleged was fairly traceable to the conduct that was claimed to be unlawful; and (3) the "separation of powers" principle does not create a jurisdictional obstacle to the consideration of the merits of Allen's (P) claim.

EDITOR'S ANALYSIS: The Supremacy Clause and the decision in Marbury v. Madison, 1 Cranch 137 (1803), plainly imply that a litigant always has standing to challenge judicial action claimed to violate his constitutional rights. Thus, in a case involving coercive action against a defendant, there is little question that he may challenge the judicial coercion as violating his rights. The purpose of standing is not only to limit relief to litigants entitled to it, but to ensure that controversies will be concrete and genuine.

NOTES:

VALLEY FORGE CHRISTIAN COLLEGE v. AMERICANS UNITED FOR SEPARATION OF CHURCH AND STATE, INC.

454 U.S. 464 (1982).

NATURE OF CASE: Appeal from reinstatement of action seeking declaration to void a conveyance of property from the United States.

FACT SUMMARY: Americans United for Separation of Church and State (P) contended they had standing as citizens to challenge the conveyance of surplus United States property to Valley Forge Christian College (D) on the ground that it violated the Establishment Clause of the First Amendment.

CONCISE RULE OF LAW: Assertion of a right to a particular kind of government conduct, which the government has violated by acting differently, is insufficient to confer standing.

FACTS: The Department of Health, Education and Welfare sold 77 acres of surplus real property to Valley Forge Christian College (D) at a discount on condition that the College (D) use the property for 30 years solely for educational purposes. Americans United (P), a group of separatists, challenged the conveyance as a violation of the Establishment Clause. They asserted that their members would be deprived of the constitutional use of their tax dollars if the conveyance were allowed to stand. The district court dismissed the complaint for lack of standing as taxpayers. The appeals court, however, reversed, concluding that Americans United (P) had standing to sue, not as taxpayers, but as citizens claiming injury in fact to their shared right to a government that "shall make no law respecting the establishment of religion." Valley Forge Christian College (D) appealed, and the Supreme Court granted certiorari.

ISSUE: Is assertion of a right to a particular kind of government conduct, which the government has violated by acting differently, sufficient to confer standing?

HOLDING AND DECISION: (Rehnquist, J.) No. Assertion of a right to a particular kind of government conduct, which the government has violated by acting differently, is insufficient to confer standing. Americans United (P) have not alleged any personal injury they have suffered as a result of HEW's property transfer; in fact they have not alleged an injury of any kind, economic or otherwise, sufficient to confer standing. The enforcement of the Establishment Clause does not exempt plaintiffs from standing requirements. Reversed.

DISSENT: (Brennan, J.) This decision is typical of the unfortunate trend of resolving cases at the threshold while obscuring the nature of the underlying rights and interests at stake.

EDITOR'S ANALYSIS: Taxpayer standing, although denied to Americans United (P) in the above case, may be a sole basis for standing, provided the plaintiff meets the test first articulated in Flast v. Cohen, 392 U.S. 83 (1968). The Flast test consists of two prongs: (1) the plaintiff must show that the challenged statute is an exercise of the congressional spending power; and (2) that the expenditure violated a specific rather than a general limitation on that power. Justice Rehnquist distinguished the Americans United case from Flast by holding the land transfer at issue was an administrative agency's actions rather than congressional legislation and made pursuant to the property clause of Article IV, rather than under the Article I spending power.

NOTES:

DeFUNIS v. ODEGAARD

416 U.S. 312 (1974).

NATURE OF CASE: Appeal from reversal of issuance of injunction.

FACT SUMMARY: DeFunis (P) who was admitted to the school while this action was pending, contended that the procedures and criteria employed by the Admissions Committee insidiously discriminated against him because of race.

CONCISE RULE OF LAW: A case is moot if the controversy between the parties has clearly ceased to be definite and concrete and no longer touches the legal relations of parties having adverse legal interests.

FACTS: DeFunis (P) applied for admission as a first-year student at the University of Washington Law School, a state-operated institution. DeFunis was eventually notified that he was denied admission. He sued Odegaard (D) and the University Law School Admissions Committee for violation of the Equal Protection Clause of the Fourteenth Amendment. DeFunis (P) contended that the procedures and criteria employed by the University insidiously discriminated against him because of his race. DeFunis (P) asked the trial court to issue a mandatory injunction commanding Odegaard (D) et al. to admit him on the grounds that the admissions policy resulted in the unconstitutional denial of his application for admission. The trial court agreed with DeFunis (P) and granted the requested relief. DeFunis (P) was admitted to the law school while Odegaard (D) appealed. The Washington Supreme Court reversed, holding that the school's admission policy did not violate the Constitution. DeFunis (P) then petitioned the U.S. Supreme Court for a writ of certiorari staying the judgment of the Washington Supreme Court pending final disposition by the U.S. Supreme Court. The writ was granted, and DeFunis (P), who remained in law school, was in the first term of his third and final year when the Court granted his petition.

ISSUE: Is a case moot if the controversy between the parties has clearly ceased to be definite and concrete and no longer touches the legal relations of parties having adverse legal interests?

HOLDING AND DECISION: (Per curiam) Yes. A case is moot if the controversy between the parties has clearly ceased to be definite and concrete and no longer touches the legal relations of the parties having adverse legal interests. Here, DeFunis (P) will complete his studies at the end of the term for which he has now registered regardless of any decision this Court might reach of the merits of the litigation. Because of this fact, the Court cannot, consistently with the limitations of Article III of the Constitution, consider the substantive constitutional issues tendered by the parties. Accordingly, the judgment of the Supreme Court of Washington is vacated, and the cause is remanded for such proceedings as that court may deem appropriate.

DISSENT: (Brennan, J.) Mere voluntary cessation of allegedly illegal conduct does not moot a case. Although the Court should, of course, avoid unnecessary decisions of constitutional questions, it should not transform principles of avoidance of constitutional decisions into devices for sidestepping resolution of difficult cases like this one.

EDITOR'S ANALYSIS: The doctrine of mootness is closely related to those of standing and ripeness. If a controversy is not judged ripe, the Court is saying that it is too early for a party claiming injury to seek relief. If the controversy is judged to be moot, the court is saying that it is too late — that because the matter has been resolved, or for other reasons, the party no longer has a claim for redress.

NOTES:

PACIFIC GAS & ELECTRIC CO. v. STATE ENERGY RESOURCES CONSERV. & DEV. COMM.

397 U.S. 150 (1970).

NATURE OF CASE: Appeal from judgment holding waste disposal regulations preempted by federal law.

FACT SUMMARY: The Ninth Circuit Court of Appeals held that a challenge to California's regulations requiring adequate storage for spent nuclear fuel was not ripe for review, but that a challenge to a moratorium on new nuclear plant certification was.

CONCISE RULE OF LAW: The question of ripeness turns on the fitness of the issues for judicial decision and the hardship to the parties of withholding court consideration.

FACTS: California adopted new regulations in 1976 dealing with new nuclear power plant construction. Section 25524.1(b) of the law, known as the interim storage provision, required the Energy Commission (D) to determine if a nuclear plant had enough capacity to store spent fuel rods before allowing the plant to be built. Section 25524.2, the moratorium provision, stated that no new nuclear plants could be certified until the Energy Commission (D) determined that there was a way to dispose of the waste. Pacific Gas & Electric Co. (P) sued to have the provisions invalidated on the grounds that they were preempted by federal law. The district court agreed. The Ninth Circuit, however, concluded that the challenge to the interim storage provision was not ripe for review. Pacific Gas (P) appealed, and the Supreme Court granted certiorari.

ISSUE: Does the question of ripeness turn on the fitness of the issues for judicial decision and the hardship to the parties of withholding court consideration?

HOLDING AND DECISION: (White, J.) Yes. The question of ripeness turns on the fitness of the issues for judicial decision and the hardship to the parties of withholding court consideration. The basic rationale behind the ripeness doctrine is to prevent the courts from entangling themselves in abstract disagreements over administrative policies and to protect the agencies from premature judicial interference. In this case, the moratorium provision is ripe because the industry would be hard-pressed to proceed with long-range construction plans without knowing whether the moratorium was valid. Conversely, the interim storage provision is not ripe for review because the Energy Commission (D) will be making its findings on a case-by-case basis and may never find a plant's storage capacity to be inadequate. Therefore, the Court should not stretch to reach a premature decision concerning its constitutionality. Affirmed.

EDITOR'S ANALYSIS: An issue that is ripe for review is sufficiently mature and crystallized to enable a court to examine the dispute arising from it. But a court cannot be expected to decide complicated technical questions; that would invade the province of the administrative agencies. A court will, however, inquire whether a determination made by an agency was procedurally correct, adequately explained, and reasonable.

NOTES:

BAKER v. CARR

369 U.S. 186 (1962).

NATURE OF CASE: Appeal from dismissal of constitutional challenge to state apportionment act.

FACT SUMMARY: The State of Tennessee (D) argued that an equal protection challenge to its method of allocating legislative representation among its counties was a nonjusticiable political question.

CONCISE RULE OF LAW: A controversy is nonjusticiable where there is a textually demonstrable constitutional commitment of the issue to a coordinate political department or a lack of judicially discoverable and manageable ways of resolving it.

FACTS: Baker (P), a resident of the state of Tennessee (D), objected to a 1901 state statute that allocated legislative representation among the counties based on the total number of qualified voters in each county. Baker (P) argued that the continued application of the 1901 Apportionment Act denied certain state citizens the equal protection of the laws because it led to "debasement" of their votes. Baker (P) sought a declaration that the 1901 statute was unconstitutional and an injunction barring its use. Tennessee (D) contended that the challenge presented a nonjusticiable political question. The district court agreed and dismissed the case. Baker (P) appealed.

ISSUE: Is a controversy nonjusticiable where there is a textually demonstrable constitutional commitment of the issue to a political department or a lack of judicially discoverable and manageable ways of resolving it?

HOLDING AND DECISION: (Brennan, J.) Yes. A controversy is nonjusticiable where there is a textually demonstrable constitutional commitment of the issue to a political department or a lack of judicially discoverable and manageable ways of resolving it. The nonjusticiability of a political question stems from a need for finality as well as from a lack of satisfactory criteria for a judicial determination. The instant issue — whether a state action is consistent with the federal Constitution — does not fall into any of the categories where the political question doctrine has been traditionally applied. There is no question to be decided by a branch of government co-equal with the Supreme Court and no foreign government or Indian tribe involved. Judicial standards under the Equal Protection Clause are well developed. Therefore, Baker's (P) allegations of a denial of equal protection under the Fourteenth Amendment present a justiciable constitutional cause of action. Reversed and remanded.

EDITOR'S ANALYSIS: The Court has continued to adjudicate equal protection claims in the legislative districting context regarding inequalities in population between districts. Racial gerrymandering has also been held to present a justiciable equal protection claim, although the Supreme Court has been deeply divided as to the justiciability of political gerrymandering. See, e.g., Davis v. Bandemer, 478 U.S. 109 (1986). In that case, a plurality of the justices maintained that any districting that would operate to minimize or cancel out the voting strength of racial or political elements of the voting population would raise a constitutional question.

NOTES:

NIXON v. UNITED STATES

___ U.S. ___, 113 S. Ct. 732 (1993).

NATURE OF CASE: Appeal from dismissal of action contesting impeachment and removal of a federal judge.

FACT SUMMARY: Following his conviction for perjury, Nixon (P), a federal district judge, was impeached by Congress and removed from office, but he insisted that he had a right to a full Senate hearing.

CONCISE RULE OF LAW: The Senate has the sole authority to determine procedures for trying an impeached official, and such procedures are unreviewable by the courts.

FACTS: Nixon (P) was a federal district judge. He was impeached by the House of Representatives after he was convicted of making false statements before a federal grand jury. Pursuant to Senate Rule XI, a committee of senators then held four days of hearings. After receiving evidence and hearing testimony, the committee presented the full Senate with a transcript of the proceeding and a summary of the evidence. Nixon (P) was allowed to make a personal appeal from the Senate floor. The full Senate then voted to impeach him, and he was removed from office. Nixon (P) filed suit, arguing that Senate Rule XI violated the constitutional grant of authority to the Senate to “try” all impeachments because it prohibited the whole Senate from taking part in the evidentiary hearings. Nixon (P) sought a declaratory judgment that his impeachment conviction was void. The district court held that his claim was nonjus-ticiable, and the court of appeals agreed. The Supreme Court granted certiorari.

ISSUE: Does the Senate have the sole authority to determine procedures for trying an impeached official, unreviewable by the courts?

HOLDING AND DECISION: (Rehnquist, C.J.) Yes. The Senate has the sole authority to determine procedures for trying an impeached official, and such procedures are unreviewable by the courts. The Impeachment Trial Clause of the U.S. Constitution provides: “The Senate shall have the sole Power to try all Impeachments.” It also specifies that the Senate shall be on oath or affirmation, that a two-thirds vote is required to convict and that, when the President is tried, the Chief Justice shall preside. Because these limitations are so precise, it may be inferred that the Framers did not intend to impose additional limitations on the form of the Senate proceedings when they inserted the word “try” in the first sentence. They envisioned two separate proceedings for those who commit impeachable offenses: the impeachment proceedings and a criminal trial. The judiciary was to have no role in the former in order to avoid the risk of bias. In addition, judicial review of impeachment procedures would be inconsistent with the Framers' insistence on a system of checks and balances. Therefore the Senate has the final authority to determine the meaning of the word “try” in the Impeachment Trial Clause. Affirmed.

EDITOR'S ANALYSIS: In a concurrence not excerpted in the casebook, Justice Souter agreed that the issue as to whether there was a constitutional infirmity in Nixon's (P) impeachment was a political question. However, he also stated, “If the Senate were to act in a manner seriously threatening the integrity of its results, convicting, say, upon a coin-toss ... judicial interference might well be appropriate. In such circumstances, the Senate's action might be so far beyond the scope of its constitutional authority, and the consequent impact on the Republic so great, as to merit a judicial response despite the prudential concerns that would ordinarily counsel silence.”

NOTES:

CHAPTER 2
CONGRESSIONAL POWER TO CONTROL FEDERAL JURISDICTION

QUICK REFERENCE RULES OF LAW

1. **Case or Controversy.** Congress has the power to remove a case or controversy from the jurisdiction of the federal courts. (Sheldon v. Sill)

2. **Congressional Power.** The congressional power to establish inferior federal courts includes the power to invest them with limited, concurrent, or exclusive jurisdiction. (Lockerty v. Phillips)

3. **Process for Challenge of Regulations.** The validity of a regulation may not be challenged in defense of a prosecution for its violation when it has not been tested by the prescribed administrative procedure and complaint to the Emergency Court of Appeals. (Yakus v. United States)

4. **Judicial Review.** Congress must allow some opportunity for an aggrieved claimant to obtain judicial review of one of its enactments. (Bartlett v. Bowen)

5. **State Court Jurisdiction.** A state court has no jurisdiction to issue a writ of habeas corpus releasing a person held by the United States or one of its officers. (Tarble's Case)

6. **Depriving the Court of Jurisdiction.** Since Congress may enact legislation concerning the appellate power of the Supreme Court, it may also repeal such laws thereby depriving the Court of jurisdiction as though the Act had not been passed. (Ex parte McCardle)

7. **De Novo Review by Federal Courts.** Although Congress may, by a specific statute, vest fact-finding authority in a tribunal other than a court, the facts that purportedly establish the applicability of such a statute to a particular case may be reviewed de novo by a federal court. (Crowell v. Benson)

8. **Article III.** Congress may expand the jurisdiction of the federal courts by enacting statutes that allow those courts to exercise jurisdiction over cases and controversies other than those enumerated in Article III of the Constitution. (National Mutual Insurance Co. v. Tidewater Transfer Co., Inc.)

NOTES

SHELDON v. SILL
8 How. 440 (1850).

NATURE OF CASE: Action to recover on a bond and mortgage.

NOTES:

FACT SUMMARY: Sheldon (D) executed a bond and mortgage. Hastings assigned both to Sill (P), a citizen of another state, who then sued in federal court to recover on the bond and mortgage.

CONCISE RULE OF LAW: Congress has the power to remove a case or controversy from the jurisdiction of the federal courts.

FACTS: Sheldon (D), a Michigan citizen, executed a bond and mortgage obligating him to the Bank of Michigan. Hastings, president of the bank, assigned the obligations to Sill (P), a resident of New York, who sued Sheldon (D) in federal court to recover on the bond and mortgage. By way of defense, Sheldon (D) cited a provision of the Judiciary Act which denied federal courts the jurisdiction to consider suits by assignees of choses in action unless the assignor could also have sued in federal court. Sill (P) countered with the observation that Article III of the Constitution vests the federal courts with jurisdiction to decide "controversies between citizens of different states." The trial court rendered judgment in favor of Sill (P), but Sheldon (D) appealed.

ISSUE: May a federal statute restrict the jurisdiction which is conferred on the federal courts by Article III of the Constitution?

HOLDING AND DECISION: (Grier, J.) Yes. Congress has the power to remove a case or controversy from the jurisdiction of the federal courts. The lower federal courts were created by Congress, not by the Constitution. Since Congress established these courts, it has the power to determine the scope of their jurisdiction. It has long been recognized that it has the right to do so by restricting the authority conferred by Article III of the Constitution, which may be construed as applying only to the Supreme Court anyway, since the Constitution set up no system of subordinate federal courts. Therefore, the cited provision of the Judiciary Act requires reversal of the judgment in favor of Sill (P) since he satisfies the Act's definition of an assignee of a chose of action.

EDITOR'S ANALYSIS: Surprisingly, some of the earliest constitutional scholars argued that Article III required Congress to vest the inferior federal courts with jurisdiction to resolve all suits enumerated in the Article. This view, however, never achieved preeminence. Today, the authority of Congress to enact laws circumscribing the jurisdiction of the federal courts is seldom questioned. In fact, Congress has frequently acted to deprive the federal courts of jurisdiction over suits which they would otherwise have the authority to decide. One way that Congress accomplishes this objective is to confer original jurisdiction to resolve certain cases upon the Supreme Court.

LOCKERTY v. PHILLIPS

319 U.S. 182 (1943).

NATURE OF CASE: Appeal from dismissal of action to enjoin criminal proceedings for violation of the Price Control Act.

FACT SUMMARY: Lockerty (P) challenged, as unconstitutional, the Emergency Price Control Act's requirement that anyone seeking to challenge a price regulation must first follow an administrative procedure and then seek review in the Emergency Court of Appeals.

CONCISE RULE OF LAW: The congressional power to establish inferior federal courts includes the power to invest them with limited, concurrent, or exclusive jurisdiction.

FACTS: United States Attorney Phillips (D) threatened to criminally prosecute Lockerty (P) for selling meat at prices exceeding current price regulations. Lockerty (P) sued in district court to enjoin Phillips (D) from prosecution on the grounds that prices fixed under the Emergency Price Control Act were so low that they amounted to a denial of due process and involved an unconstitutional delegation of legislative power to the Price Administrator. The district court dismissed the suit after concluding that Lockerty (P) should have filed first a protest with the Administrator as provided by the Act and, if not satisfied, then filed a complaint with the Emergency Court of Appeals created pursuant to the Act. Lockerty (P) appealed, arguing that because the Act itself prohibited any courts from determining the constitutionality of any provision of the Act, he was denied his day in court to challenge its constitutionality.

ISSUE: Does the congressional power to establish inferior federal courts include the power to invest them with limited, concurrent, or exclusive jurisdiction?

HOLDING AND DECISION: (Stone, C.J.) Yes. The congressional power to establish inferior federal courts includes the power to invest them with limited, concurrent, or exclusive jurisdiction. In this case, Congress has conferred on the Emergency Court equity jurisdiction to restrain the enforcement of price orders under the Emergency Price Control Act. It has simultaneously withdrawn that jurisdiction from every other federal and state court. Article III of the Constitution left Congress free to establish inferior federal courts as it thought appropriate. Therefore, Congress has the authority to restrict enforcement of the Act to the Emergency Court and also to require Lockerty (P) to resort to the Emergency Court only after pursuing the prescribed administrative procedure. The Emergency Court, in turn, is empowered by the Act to determine whether any orders or regulations involving an unconstitutional application of the Act are not in accordance with law. Since the Act withholds from the district courts the authority to enjoin enforcement of the Act, and Lockerty (P) sought an injunction that the district court does not have the authority to give, his suit was properly dismissed. Affirmed.

EDITOR'S ANALYSIS: As this decision explains, all federal courts, other than the Supreme Court, derive their jurisdiction wholly from the exercise of the authority to "ordain and establish" inferior courts conferred on Congress by Article III, § 1, of the Constitution. The power to ordain and establish includes the power to withhold jurisdiction from them as Congress may see fit. Some legal commentators have maintained that such courts may therefore be abolished altogether by Congress, or at least be prohibited from considering certain issues by removing those areas from their jurisdiction.

NOTES:

YAKUS v. UNITED STATES

321 U.S. 414 (1944).

NATURE OF CASE: Appeal from conviction for violation of the Emergency Price Control Act.

FACTS: Yakus (P) raised the defense of invalidity of a price regulation promulgated under the Emergency Price Control Act during his trial for selling beef at prices above the maximum prices set pursuant to the Act.

CONCISE RULE OF LAW: The validity of a regulation may not be challenged in defense of a prosecution for its violation when it has not been tested by the prescribed administrative procedure and complaint to the Emergency Court of Appeals.

FACTS: Yakus (P) was tried and convicted of violating the Emergency Price Control Act by selling beef at more than the maximum price regulation. Prior to trial, Yakus (P) did not avail himself of the procedures prescribed in the Act for protesting the validity of a regulation — i.e., an appeal to the Price Administrator and review by the Emergency Court of Appeals. During the trial, Yakus (P) challenged the regulation as invalid and unconstitutional. The district court rejected all challenges and convicted Yakus (P). The appeals court affirmed. Yakus (P) appealed, and the Supreme Court granted certiorari.

ISSUE: May the validity of a regulation be challenged in defense of a prosecution for its violation when it has not been tested by the prescribed administrative procedure and complaint to the Emergency Court of Appeals?

HOLDING AND DECISION: (Stone, C.J.) No. The validity of a regulation may not be challenged in defense of a prosecution for its violation when it has not been tested by the prescribed administrative procedure and complaint to the Emergency Court of Appeals. The procedure that Congress has established for determining the validity of the Administrator's price regulations is exclusive so as to preclude the defense of invalidity of the regulation in this criminal prosecution. Yakus (P) did not seek the administrative remedy and the statutory review open to him, a procedure that would have protected his rights as required by due process. Even though the Act denies interlocutory relief pending a judicial determination of the regulation's validity, this is a constitutional choice made by Congress and does not constitute a denial of due process. Affirmed.

DISSENT: (Rutledge, J.) Congress may not constitutionally provide one proceeding for deciding upon the validity of a law or regulation with a 60-day deadline and then cut off all other rights to question the proceeding, as it has done here.

EDITOR'S ANALYSIS: Justice Rutledge, in his dissent, conceded that Congress could legitimately confer exclusive jurisdiction upon the Emergency Court of Appeals to determine the validity of price regulations. It could also deprive other federal courts of jurisdiction to issue stay orders, injunctions, or other relief to prevent the operation of price regulations or to set them aside. What it could not do, he believed, especially in the context of a criminal prosecution involving rights of liberty and life, was permit federal and state courts to enforce the Act while simultaneously denying them the power to consider the validity of the regulations for which enforcement was being sought.

NOTES:

BARTLETT v. BOWEN

816 F.2d 695 (D.C. Cir. 1987).

NATURE OF CASE: Appeal from dismissal of constitutional challenge to the Medicare Act.

FACT SUMMARY: Bartlett (P) contended that Congress did not intend to bar judicial review of constitutional challenges to the Medicare Act.

CONCISE RULE OF LAW: Congress must allow some opportunity for an aggrieved claimant to obtain judicial review of one of its enactments.

FACTS: Bartlett (P) challenged the constitutionality of the Medicare Act on the ground that its partial bar to payment of benefits burdened the free exercise of her sister's Christian Science faith. The district court dismissed the claim because it did not meet the $1,000 amount in controversy required by the Medicare Act for judicial review of benefit decisions. Bartlett (P) appealed, arguing that the Medicare Act did not preclude judicial review of her constitutional claim or, if it did, such a provision denied her due process and equal protection of the law.

ISSUE: Must Congress allow some opportunity for an aggrieved claimant to obtain judicial review of one of its enactments?

HOLDING AND DECISION: (Edwards, J.) Yes. Congress must allow some opportunity for an aggrieved claimant to obtain judicial review of one of its enactments. In this case, Congress did not intend to preclude judicial review of Bartlett's (P) claim. Furthermore, Congress may not, as the dissent suggests, insist on sovereign immunity as a way to foreclose all judicial review of its own actions. There appears to be a due process right to have the scope of constitutional rights determined by some independent judicial body. To permit Congress to foreclose all judicial review would be flatly inconsistent with the doctrine of separation of powers. Reversed.

DISSENT: (Bork, J.) Sovereign immunity denies the district court jurisdiction to entertain Bartlett's (P) claim. Benefit claims like this one constitute the category of cases in which sovereign immunity is most readily upheld.

EDITOR'S ANALYSIS: The Supreme Court has stated "that where Congress intends to preclude judicial review of constitutional claims its intent to do so must be clear." Webster v. Doe, 486 U.S. 592, 603 (1988). Justice Scalia, echoing Justice Bork's dissent above, disagreed that such a heightened showing was required. He argued that there did not need to be a judicial remedy for every constitutional violation, just as some claims are found to be beyond judicial review because they involve political questions.

NOTES:

TARBLE'S CASE

80 U.S. (13 Wall.) 397 (1871).

NATURE OF CASE: Petition for a writ of habeas corpus.

FACT SUMMARY: Tarble, a minor, enlisted in the United States (D) Army without his father's (P) consent. The father (P) then petitioned for a writ of habeas corpus to obtain the minor's release from the service.

CONCISE RULE OF LAW: A state court has no jurisdiction to issue a writ of habeas corpus releasing a person held by the United States or one of its officers.

FACTS: Edward Tarble enlisted in the United States to obtain his father's (P) consent to enlist. Asserting these facts, Tarble's father (P) petitioned the Dane County, Wisconsin, court for a writ of habeas corpus directing the United States (D) to release his son. A commissioner of that court granted the writ, and the Supreme Court of Wisconsin ultimately affirmed the validity of its issuance. The United States (D) then brought a writ of error, challenging the jurisdiction of the state court to issue the writ in question.

ISSUE: May a state court issue a writ of habeas corpus releasing a person from the custody of the United States government?

HOLDING AND DECISION: No. A state court has no jurisdiction to issue a writ of habeas corpus releasing a person held by the United States or one of its officers. State and local governments conflict in some spheres, but the Constitution provides that when jurisdictional confrontations occur, it is the federal government that decides. The harmonious interrelating of the two levels of government requires that the authority of one yield to the other, and it is the state that must give way. The federal government has plenary authority to maintain and regulate the military, and if state judicial officers had the power to secure the release of soldiers, the effectiveness of the army would be drastically undermined. To deprive states of the power to issue writs of habeas corpus against the United States (D) in no way threatens civil liberties because the federal government is as jealous a protector of individual rights as any state government. If, however, the relief sought in this case were permitted, the United States (D) would face endless challenges to its authority and would continually have to involve itself in protracted legal proceedings in order to preserve the effectiveness of the military. For these reasons, the Dane County court had no jurisdiction to issue the writ of habeas corpus releasing Tarble.

DISSENT: (Chief J. Chase) The Constitution gives state courts the right to issue writs of habeas corpus against the United States government, although their decisions to do so are, of course, ultimately reviewable by the Supreme Court. If state courts are denied the power to issue such writs, many injustices and errors in judgment will go unrectified.

EDITOR'S ANALYSIS: Prior to Tarble's case, state courts had frequently asserted a right to issue writs of habeas corpus to release individuals from the custody of the United States. Some state courts appear to have continued the practice even after the Tarble decision. The reasoning of Tarble's case has been expanded to apply to other writs as well. For example, in McClung v. Sillman, 6 Wheat. 598 (U.S. 1821), it was held that a writ of mandamus could not issue from a state court to compel action on the part of a register of the United States land office. The McClung decision was premised on the fact that the United States had not even given federal courts the power to issue writs of mandamus against an executive official, but the case has traditionally been interpreted as barring state mandamus under any circumstances.

NOTES:

EX PARTE McCARDLE

7 Wall. 506, 19 L.Ed. 264.

NATURE OF CASE: Appeal from an action for a writ of habeas corpus.

FACT SUMMARY: McCardle (D), a civilian taken into military custody for alleged libelous news articles was denied a writ of habeas corpus to the Supreme Court under a Congressional Act which restricted the Court's jurisdiction.

CONCISE RULE OF LAW: Since Congress may enact legislation concerning the appellate power of the Supreme Court, it may also repeal such laws thereby depriving the Court of jurisdiction as though the Act had not been passed.

FACTS: McCardle (D) was a civilian newspaper editor who was taken into military custody for alleged libelous news articles. McCardle (D) was brought before a military commission pursuant to Civil War Reconstruction Statutes. Upon a hearing McCardle (D) was remanded to military custody and allowed to appeal to the Supreme Court under the Act of 1967. This Act granted to the federal courts power to issue writs of habeas corpus in all cases where a person may be restrained of his liberty in violation of the Constitution or any treaty or law of the United States from which appeal could be taken to the Supreme Court. The Supreme Court granted jurisdiction for an appeal on the merits. However, while the appeal was pending, Congress passed another Act in 1 868 which repealed the 1867 Act. Consequently, the Supreme Court dismissed the appeal for want of jurisdiction.

ISSUE: Does the Constitution grant to Congress the power to effect the appellate jurisdiction of the Supreme Court and thus deprive the Court of jurisdiction?

HOLDING AND DECISION: (The Chief Justice) Yes. Although the appellate jurisdiction of the Supreme Court is not derived from Acts of Congress, but is conferred by the Constitution, it is conferred with such exceptions and under such regulations as Congress shall make. Thus the effect of the repealing act on the case at bar is to deny to the Supreme Court jurisdiction in habeas corpus cases. When an act of the legislature is repealed, it must be considered, except as to transactions past and closed, as if it never existed. The effect of repealing acts upon suits under acts repealed is that no judgment can be rendered. Therefore, it is clear that this court cannot proceed to pronounce judgment, for it no longer has jurisdiction of the appeal. The appeal is dismissed.

EDITOR'S ANALYSIS: In the case at bar the Supreme Court considered it immaterial that the repealing act was passed after the Court had already taken jurisdiction. Although the McCardle case is usually interpreted as granting to Congress full power over the appellate jurisdiction of the Supreme Court, there has been some suggestion of late that this might be too broad an interpretation. That is to say, it is argued that this broad power of Congress does not extend to such exceptions as might destroy the primary functions of the Supreme Court in the constitutional scheme. Reinforcing this suggestion is the fact that shortly after the McCardle case it was held in Ex Parte Yerger that review of cases such as McCardle might be accomplished under the Supreme Court's power to issue original writs of habeas corpus and certiorari.

NOTES:

CROWELL v. BENSON

285 U.S. 22 (1932).

NATURE OF CASE: Suit to enjoin enforcement of an award made by an administrative agency.

FACT SUMMARY: Crowell (P), Deputy Commissioner of a government agency, ordered Benson (D) to compensate Knudsen (P) for an injury allegedly suffered by Knudsen (P) while in Benson's (D) employ.

CONCISE RULE OF LAW: Although Congress may, by a specific statute, vest fact-finding authority in a tribunal other than a court, the facts that purportedly establish the applicability of such a statute to a particular case may be reviewed de novo by a federal court.

FACTS: Knudsen (P) filed a claim under the Longshoremen's and Harbor Workers' Compensation Act, claiming that he had been injured while in the employ of Benson (D). Crowell (P), as Deputy Commissioner of the United States Employees' Compensation Commission, made an award in Knudsen's (P) favor, but Benson (D), contending that Knudsen (P) had not been in his employ at the time of the injury, brought suit to enjoin the enforcement of the award. The federal district court granted a hearing de novo upon both the law and the facts. That court eventually determined that Knudsen (P) had not been in Benson's (D) employ and restrained the enforcement of the award. The Circuit Court of Appeals affirmed. Crowell (P) petitioned for certiorari to the United States Supreme Court, and Benson (D) argued that the Compensation Act, which gave judicial authority to Crowell (P) as Deputy Commissioner, was violative of the constitutional guarantees of due process and trial by jury as well as the provisions of Article III of the Constitution pertaining to the judicial power of the United States. Crowell (P) argued that the award in favor of Knudsen (P) should not have been overturned and that the court should not have conducted a de novo review of the facts upon which Knudsen's (P) claim was based.

ISSUE: May a federal district court conduct a de novo review of the factual basis for a decision rendered, pursuant to congressional authorization, by an administrative agency?

HOLDING AND DECISION: (Hughes, J.) Yes. Although Congress may, by a specific statute, vest fact-finding authority in a tribunal other than a court, the facts which purportedly establish the applicability of such a statute to a particular case may be reviewed de novo by a federal court. There are sound reasons why Congress might have desired the Deputy Commissioner's (P) factual conclusions to be final. On the other hand, the issue of whether or not Knudsen (P) was in Benson's (D) employ was "jurisdictional" in the sense that, unless that fact could be established, the Compensation Act could not have become operative and the Deputy Commissioner (P) could not have conducted the judicial hearing in the first place. Review of this factual determination was within the purview of the court, from which it follows that it was proper for the district court to conduct a hearing de novo. Moreover, the evidence adduced at the hearing amply supports the conclusion that the award in Knudsen's (P) favor should not have been made because he was not in Benson's (D) employ at the time of his injury.

DISSENT: (Brandeis, J.) The Deputy Commissioner (P) necessarily determined that an employer-employee relationship existed, and his determination in that respect should be accorded finality. There is no constitutional impediment to denying a de novo review of the Deputy Commissioner's (P) findings.

EDITOR'S ANALYSIS: Crowell v. Benson illustrates the principle that Congress may, by the enactment of a particular statute, deprive the federal courts of jurisdiction over types of cases which would otherwise be within the ambit of their authority. Legislative functions are frequently conferred upon administrative agencies, although the Administrative Procedure Act generally accords a right to judicial review of administrative decision. In addition, Congress sometimes passes over the lower federal courts and gives the Supreme Court exclusive jurisdiction over matters that would otherwise be cognizable in a federal district court, and other courts are also occasionally given jurisdiction over matters after Congress has specifically removed them from the authority of the lower federal courts.

NOTES:

NATIONAL MUTUAL INSURANCE v. TIDEWATER TRANSFER CO., INC.

337 U.S. 582 (1949).

NATURE OF CASE: Suit seeking damages pursuant to a claim based on an insurance contract.

FACT SUMMARY: National (P), a District of Columbia corporation, sued Tidewater (D), a corporation licensed to do business in Maryland, in the federal district court for Maryland, alleging diversity of citizenship.

CONCISE RULE OF LAW: Congress may expand the jurisdiction of the federal courts by enacting statutes that allow those courts to exercise jurisdiction over cases and controversies other than those enumerated in Article III of the Constitution.

FACTS: National Mutual (P), a corporation created under the laws of the District of Columbia, sued Tidewater Transfer (D) for damages based on an insurance contract. The suit was filed in the federal district court of Maryland, where Tidewater (D) was licensed to do business, and alleged diversity of citizenship as the basis for federal jurisdiction. Tidewater (D) contended that a citizen of the District of Columbia could not sue in a federal district court located in one of the states if he based jurisdiction solely on diversity of citizenship. The district court judge agreed and dismissed the action. His judgment was affirmed by a divided Court of Appeals. The Supreme Court then granted certiorari, and National Mutual (P) argued that a valid federal statute authorized federal courts to exercise jurisdiction over a suit by a citizen of the District of Columbia against a citizen of a state.

ISSUE: May Congress enact statutes that extend the jurisdiction of the federal court s to cases and controversies other than those specified in Article III of the Constitution?

HOLDING AND DECISION: (Jackson, J.) Yes. Congress may expand the jurisdiction of the federal courts by enacting statutes that allow those courts to exercise jurisdiction over cases and controversies other than those enumerated in Article III of the Constitution. It was long ago settled that Article III's grant of federal jurisdiction in all cases involving suits between citizens of different states does not apply to actions prosecuted by citizens of the District of Columbia because that municipality is not a state. However, Congress in 1940 expressly authorized the federal courts to exercise jurisdiction over suits maintained by a citizen of the District of Columbia against a citizen of any state. The constitutionality of this enactment should be beyond doubt because Article I gives Congress the power to increase the jurisdiction of Article III courts. In may instances in the past, Article I has, in fact, been invoked as a basis for conferring additional jurisdiction on those courts. Congress has the power to permit suits of the type in this case to be maintained in the federal district court sitting in the District of Columbia. It would be ludicrous to hold that such actions may not also be prosecuted in the federal court located in the defendant's home state, a forum which will virtually always be a more convenient one for the defendant. The courts below should have upheld the validity of the statute relied upon by National (P) and should have permitted the present action to be maintained in the federal district court in Maryland.

CONCURRENCE: (Rutledge, J.) The majority opinion is unsatisfactory to the extent that it states that Article I confers upon Congress the authority to vest Article III courts with legislative jurisdiction.

DISSENT: (Vinson, J.) The framers of the Constitution clearly intended that federal courts should have jurisdiction over only those cases expressly enumerated in Article III. The federalist scheme did not contemplate that Congress should have the power, at any time, to expand the jurisdiction of those courts. The jurisdiction of Article III courts may always be limited by Congress, and so-called legislative courts may assume jurisdiction over cases formerly cognizable before constitutional courts. The two types of courts may even exercise concurrent jurisdiction over certain types of cases. But Congress may never expand the jurisdiction of the Article III courts, considerations of expediency and convenience notwithstanding.

DISSENT: (Frankfurter, J.) Congress should not be permitted to tamper with a passage so explicit as that by which Article III delineates the types of cases and controversies over which the federal courts are entitled to assume jurisdiction. If Congress may once expand the jurisdiction of Article III courts, it could in the future vest those courts with jurisdiction in other contexts with undesirable consequences. The constitutional Convention and its members were, in many ways, distrustful of the federal courts, and were especially reluctant to adopt the concept of diversity jurisdiction. Congress should not be permitted to expand the jurisdiction of the very courts that the framers so purposefully endeavored to limit in authority.

EDITOR'S ANALYSIS: One may mount fairly persuasive arguments, if not compelling ones, in support of the conclusion reached by Justice Jackson. Congress has the power to enact laws concerning the governing of the nation's capitol and could presumably pass laws pertaining to the substantive rights and legal relations of District of Columbia citizens. Whatever statutes Congress passed toward this end would unquestionably qualify as federal laws. Thus, any litigation involving such legislation would present a federal question obviating the need for a plaintiff to establish diversity of citizenship. Nevertheless, the majority opinion authored by Justice Jackson has been attacked by commentators, and it should be noted that his opinion was joined in by only two other members of the court.

CHAPTER 3
LEGISLATIVE COURTS

QUICK REFERENCE RULES OF LAW

1. **Article III.** Article III of the U.S. Constitution bars Congress from establishing legislative courts to exercise jurisdiction over all matters relating to those arising under bankruptcy laws. (Northern Pipeline Construction Co. v. Marathon Pipe Line Co.)

2. **The Commodity Exchange Act.** The broad grant of power in 7 U.S.C. § 12a(5), the Commodity Exchange Act, clearly authorizes promulgation of regulations providing for adjudication of common low counterclaims arising out of the some transaction as a reparations complaint. (Commodity Futures Trading Commission v. Schor)

NOTES

NORTHERN PIPELINE CONSTRUCTION CO. v. MARATHON PIPELINE CO.
456 U.S. 50 (1984).

NATURE OF CASE: Appeal from dismissal of action for damages for breach of contract.

FACT SUMMARY: When Northern Pipeline Construction Co. (P) initiated bankruptcy proceedings in district court and then filed suit in that same court against Marathon Pipeline Co. (D) for damages arising from breach of contract, Marathon (D) sought dismissal of the suit on the grounds that a bankruptcy judge did not have the authority to try the damages action.

CONCISE RULE OF LAW: Article III of the U.S. Constitution bars Congress from establishing legislative courts to exercise jurisdiction over all matters relating to those arising under bankruptcy laws.

FACTS: Northern Pipeline Construction Co. (P) initiated, in the U.S. Bankruptcy Court, a petition for reorganization. Northern (P) then, pursuant to the Bankruptcy Act of 1978, filed a suit in that court against Marathon Pipeline Co. (D), sinking damages for alleged breaches of contract and warranty. Marathon (D) then moved to dismiss the suit, on the ground that the Bankruptcy Act unconstitutionally conferred Article III judicial power upon judges who lacked life tenure and protection against salary diminution. The Bankruptcy Judge denied the motion to dismiss. Marathon (D) appealed, and the district court entered an order granting Marathon's (D) motion on the ground that the delegation of authority in 28 U.S.C. 1471 to the bankruptcy judges to try cases which are otherwise relegated under the Constitution to Article III judges was unconstitutional. Northern (P) appealed to the U.S. Supreme Court.

ISSUE: Does Article III of the U.S. Constitution bar Congress from establishing legislative courts to exercise jurisdiction over all matters relating to those arising under bankruptcy laws?

HOLDING AND DECISION: (Brennan, J.) Yes. Article III of the U.S. Constitution bars Congress from establishing legislative courts to exercise jurisdiction over all matters relating to those arising under bankruptcy laws. When Congress creates a statutory right, it has the discretion in defining that right to create presumptions or prescribe remedies; it may also provide that persons seeking to vindicate that right must do so before particularized tribunals created to perform the specialized adjudicative tasks related to that right. Such provisions do, in a sense, affect the exercise of judicial power, but they are also incidental to Congress' power to define the right it has created. No comparable justification exists, however, when the right being adjudicated is not of congressional creation. In such a situation, substantial inroads into functions that have traditionally been performed by the Judiciary cannot be characterized merely as incidental extensions of Congress' power to define rights that it has created. Rather, such inroads suggest unwarranted encroachments upon the judicial power of the United States, which our Constitution reserves for Article III courts. The Bankruptcy Act of 1978 carries the possibility of such an unwarranted encroachment. Many of the rights subject to adjudication by the Act's bankruptcy courts are not of Congress' creation. Indeed, the present case, which centers on Northern's (P) claim for damages for breach of contract and misrepresentation, involves a right created by state law, a right independent of and antecedent to the reorganization petition that conferred jurisdiction on the Bankruptcy Court. Accordingly, Congress' authority to control the manner in which that right is adjudicated plainly must be deemed at a minimum. Therefore, it must be concluded that Congress has impermissibly removed most, if not all of the essential attributes of the judicial power from the Article III district court and has vested them in a non-Article III adjunct. Such a grant of jurisdiction cannot be sustained as an exercise of Congress' power to create adjuncts to Article III courts. Affirmed.

CONCURRENCE: (Rehnquist, J.) None of the causes dealing with the authority of Congress to create courts other than by use of its power under Article III has gone so far as to sanction the type of adjudication to which Marathon (D) will be subjected against its will under the provisions of the 1978 Act. Adjudication of Northern's (P) lawsuit cannot, thus, be sustained.

DISSENT: (Burger, C.J.) The problems arising from today's judgment can be resolved simply by providing that ancillary law actions, such as the one involved in this case, can be routed to the United States District Court of which the bankruptcy court is an adjunct.

DISSENT: (White, J.) There is no basis for doing more than declaring § 241(a) unconstitutional as applied to the claim against Marathon (D), rather than striking down the § 241(a) grant of authority to bankruptcy courts altogether. Any attempt to distinguish Article I from Article III courts by the character of the controversies they adjudicate fundamentally misunderstands the historical and constitutional significance of Article I courts.

EDITOR'S ANALYSIS: Since the 1940's, over 100 proposals have been introduced in Congress to eliminate or restrict the jurisdiction of the federal courts. No such proposal directed at a particular Supreme Court decision or group of decisions has been enacted, though some have come close and have been the subject of much debate. In the late 1950's and in the 1960's, the proposals covered such topics as state and federal legislation regulating subversive activities, the admissibility of confessions in state criminal cases, and state legislative reapportionments.

NOTES:

COMMODITY FUTURES TRADING COMM'N v. SCHOR

478 U.S. 833 (1986).

NATURE OF CASE.: Appeal from court ruling limiting administrative jurisdiction.

FACT SUMMARY: In Schor's (P) action against the Commodity Future Trading Commission (CFTC) (D) for redress stemming from a violation of the Commodity Exchange Act by Schor's (P) stockbroker, Schor (P) contended that the CFTC (D) had no power to adjudicate a counterclaim made against Schor (P) by his broker.

CONCISE RULE OF LAW: The broad grant of power In 7 U.S.C. § 12a(5), the Commodity Exchange Act, clearly authorizes promulgation of regulations providing for adjudication of common low counterclaims arising out of the some transaction as a reparations complaint.

FACTS: Under the Commodity Exchange Act, 7 U.S.C. § 12a(5), fraudulent and manipulative conduct in connection with commodity futures transactions may be prosecuted. The Commodity Futures Trading Commission CFTC (D) was created as an independent agency with authority to implement the Act. Among the duties assigned the CTFC (D) was administration of a reparation procedure in which customers of professional brokers could seek redress for the broker's violations of the Acts or CTFC (D) regulations. The CTFC (D) then promulgated a regulation which allowed it to adjudicate counterclaims arising out of the transaction set forth in the original complaint; this regulation also allowed a counterclaimant the option in a reparations proceeding to seek relief against the reparations complainant in another forum. Schor (P) filed a complaint against his futures broker, Conti, with the CFTC (D). Schor (P) had an account with Conti which contained a debit balance because Schor's (P) net futures trading losses and expenses exceeded the funds deposited in Schor's (P) account. Schor (P) alleged that the debit balance was the result of Conti's violations of the Act. Conti brought a counterclaim against Schor (P) in the CFRC (D) and denied violating the Act, insisting that the debit balance resulted from Schor's (P) trading and was, therefore, a simple debt owed by Schor(P). The judge in the CFTC (D) proceeding ruled in Conti's favor on all claims and counterclaims. Schor (P) then challenged the CFTC's (D) statutory authority to adjudicate Conti's counterclaim, contending that the CFRC (D) had no power to adjudicate the counterclaim made against Schor (P). The CFRC (D) judge rejected Schor's (P) challenge, and the CFTC (D) declined to review the ruling. Schor (p) then filed a petition for review with the Court of Appeals. The Court dismissed Conti's counterclaims, basing its decision on the reasoning that Congress had no explicit intention of giving CFTC (D) constitutionally questionable jurisdiction over state common law counterclaims. CFRC (D) appealed.

ISSUE.: Does the broad grant of power in 7 U.S.C. § 12a(5), the Commodity Exchange Act, clearly authorize promulgation of regulations providing for adjudication of common law counterclaims arising out of the same transaction as a reparations complaint?

HOLDING AND DECISION: (O'Connor, J.) Yes. The broad grant of power in 7 U.S.C. § 12a(5), the Commodity Exchange Act, clearly authorizes promulgation of regulations providing for adjudication of common law counterclaims arising out of the same transaction as a reparations complaint. Here, under the court of appeals approach, the entire dispute may not be resolved in the administrative forum. Consequently, the entire dispute will typically end up in court, for when the broker files suit to recover the debit balance, the customer will normally be compelled either by compulsory counterclaim rules or by the expense or inconvenience of litigating the same issues in two forums to forego his reparations remedy and to litigate his claim in court. In sum, as Schor (P) himself aptly summarized, to require a bifurcated examination of the single dispute "would be to emasculate if not destroy the purposed of the Commodity Exchange Act to provide an efficient and relatively inexpensive forum for the resolution of disputes in futures trading." Thus, the CFTC's (D) longheld position that it has the power to take jurisdiction over counterclaims such as Conti's is eminently reasonable and well within the scope of its delegated authority. Reversed and remanded.

DISSENT: (Brennan, J.) By sanctioning the adjudication of state law counterclaims by a federal administrative agency, the Court exceeds the analytic framework of its precedents. Perhaps the resolution of claims such as Schor's (P) may be accomplished more conveniently under the Court's decision than under an approach which does not abdicate responsibility to legislative convenience, but the framers of the U.S. Constitution foreswore this sort of convenience in order to preserve freedom. Our Constitution unambiguously enunciates a fundamental principle that the judicial power of the United States be reposed in an independent judiciary.

EDITOR'S ANALYSIS: After the Schor decision, the black letter law would appear to be that the validity of statutes giving legislative or administrative tribunals the power to adjudicate cases arising under federal law will depend on a "balancing"of the concerns that moved Congress to choose such a "balancing" of the concerns that moved Congress to choose such a tribunal against the values embodied in Article III of the U.S. Constitution. It is obvious that this test gives Congress much latitude. Thus, the choice of a legislative or administrative tribunal is valid if Congress has made a reasoned judgment that it is necessary and proper, in connection with a valid statutory enterprise, to delegate an adjudicative function to a special or temporary tribunal or agency that is constituted without regard to the restrictions and guarantees of Article III.

NOTES:

CHAPTER 4
STATE COURTS AND FEDERAL POWER

QUICK REFERENCE RULES OF LAW

1. **Subject-matter Jurisdiction.** State courts may assume subject-matter jurisdiction over a federal cause of action absent provision by Congress to the contrary or disabling incompatibility between the federal claim and state-court adjudication. (Gulf Offshore Co. v. Mobil Oil Corp.)

2. **Federal-State Conflicts.** A state court cannot refuse to enforce a right arising from federal law for reasons of conflict with state policy or “want of wisdom” on the part of Congress. (Testa v. Katt)

3. **Federal-State Conflicts.** Though federal claims may be adjudicated by state courts, state claims are not controlling on the question of what the incidents of any federal right may be. (Dice v. Akron, Canton & Youngstown Railroad Co.)

NOTES

GULF OFFSHORE CO. v. MOBIL OIL CORP.

453 U.S. 473 (1981).

NATURE OF CASE: Appeal from award of $900,000 in negligence action.

FACT SUMMARY: Gulf Offshore Co. (D) argued that a Texas state court could not exercise jurisdiction over a personal injury action arising under the Outer Continental Shelf Lands Act since federal-court jurisdiction over operations on the Shelf was exclusive.

CONCISE RULE OF LAW: State courts may assume subject-matter jurisdiction over a federal cause of action absent provision by Congress to the contrary or disabling incompatibility between the federal claim and state-court adjudication.

FACTS: Gaedecke (P) brought suit in Texas state court against Mobil Oil Corp. (D) for injuries he suffered near an oil drilling platform above the seabed of the Outer Continental Shelf. Mobil (D) in turn filed a third-party complaint for indemnification against Gulf Offshore Co. (D). The jury found for Gaedecke (P), and the trial judge entered judgment against Gulf Offshore Co. (D) for $900,000. Gulf Offshore Co. (D) argued that the Texas district court did not have subject-matter jurisdiction over the action because the Outer Continental Shelf was an area of exclusive federal jurisdiction. The Texas appellate court disagreed, however, and affirmed the judgment. The Texas Supreme Court denied review, and the Supreme Court granted certiorari.

ISSUE: May state courts assume subject-matter jurisdiction over a federal cause of action absent provision by Congress to the contrary?

HOLDING AND DECISION: (Powell, J.) Yes. State courts may assume subject-matter jurisdiction over a federal cause of action absent provision by Congress to the contrary or disabling incompatibility between the federal claim and state-court adjudication. The presumption that state courts enjoy concurrent jurisdiction with federal courts may be rebutted by an explicit statutory directive, by unmistakable implication from legislative history, or by a clear incompatibility between state-court jurisdiction and federal interests. None of the above exceptions exist in this case. Nothing in the language, structure, legislative history, or underlying policies of OCSLA suggests that Congress intended federal courts to exercise exclusive jurisdiction over personal injury actions arising under OCSLA. Affirmed.

EDITOR'S ANALYSIS: See also Tafflin v. Levitt, 793 U.S. 455 (1990), in which the Court used the test articulated above to find that there was no clear incompatibility between state court jurisdiction over civil claims arising under the Racketeer Influenced and Corrupt Organizations Act (RICO) and federal interests. RICO, like OCSLA, was silent on the issue, and Justice O'Connor concluded that the legislative history indicated that Congress had not even considered the issue. She stated that the state courts would be guided by federal court interpretations of the relevant criminal statutes and should have no problems handling the complexities of RICO actions, since many such cases involved violations of state laws.

NOTES:

TESTA v. KATT

330 U. S. 386 (1947).

NATURE OF CASE: Appeal from reversal of an award of damages under the Emergency Price Control Act.

FACT SUMMARY: Testa (P) sought treble damages in Rhode Island State Court for Katt's (D) violation of the Federal Emergency Price Control Act for selling him an auto for more than the ceiling price.

CONCISE RULE OF LAW: A state court cannot refuse to enforce a right arising from federal law for reasons of conflict with state policy or “want of wisdom” on the part of Congress.

FACTS: Under the Emergency Price Control Act, anyone who sold goods for more than the price ceiling on those goods was liable to the buyer for treble the overcharge plus attorney fees. The federal act created a right of action not only in federal court, but in state court as well. Testa (P) purchased a car in 1944 from Katt (D), a dealer, for $1,100, $210 above the ceiling price. Testa (P) brought suit under the act in Providence, Rhode Island, in the State District Court. He was awarded the full amount of damages possible under the act. On appeal to the State Superior Court, damages were reduced to the amount of overcharge plus fees. The State Supreme Court reversed on grounds that the federal statute was penal, and that it need not enforce penal laws of a government foreign in the international sense. It held that, as the United States was foreign in the “private international” sense, it need not enforce the federal Act. Testa (P) appealed.

ISSUE: Can a state court refuse to enforce a right arising from federal law for reasons of conflict with state policy or “want of wisdom” on part of Congress?

HOLDING AND DECISION: (Black, J.) No. A state court cannot refuse to enforce a right arising from federal law for reasons of conflict with state policy or “want of wisdom” on part of Congress. The supremacy clause of the Constitution provides that the Constitution, federal law and treaties are the supreme law of the land, that the judges in every state are bound by that supreme law, any state law, Constitution, or policy to the contrary notwithstanding. The obligation of states to enforce federal laws is not lessened by reason of the form in which they are cast or the remedy which they provide. For a state to say that federal policy is in conflict with its own proscribed enforcement of the federal act is to ignore the policy espoused by Congress for all the people and all the states. Rhode Island's failure to enforce the federal act violated the supremacy clause and necessitates reversal. Reversed and remanded.

EDITOR'S ANALYSIS: A state court must entertain a cause of action created under federal law providing jurisdiction in state courts. States may not discriminate against rights that arise under federal laws. Despite the rule of this case, the question left unanswered is, where did Congress obtain the power to require state courts to exercise jurisdiction? Some suggest the Necessary and Proper Clause as the source for such power while others have inferred it to come from Congress' power to establish inferior courts.

NOTES:

DICE v. AKRON, CANTON & YOUNGSTOWN R.R. CO.

342 U.S. 359 (1952).

NATURE OF CASE: Negligence action under the Federal Employer's Liability Act.

FACT SUMMARY: Dice (P), a railroad fireman, was injured in an accident involving one of Akron, Canton & Youngstown R.R. Co.'s (D) trains.

CONCISE RULE OF LAW: Though federal claims may be adjudicated by state courts, state claims are not controlling on the question of what the incidents of any federal right may be.

FACTS: Dice (P), a railroad fireman, was injured when an engine of the Railroad (D) jumped the track. He sued in an Ohio state court under the Federal Employers Liability Act, charging negligence. At trial, the Railroad (D) offered in defense a document signed by Dice (P) which purported to release the Railroad (D) of all liability over and above $924.63 which Dice (P) had already received. Dice (P) contended that he had not read the statement before signing it, relying on fraudulent representations of the Railroad (D) that the document was merely a receipt for the $924.63. The jury found for Dice (P), but the trial court entered "judgment notwithstanding the verdict" for the Railroad (D) on the grounds that under Ohio state law Dice (P) could not escape responsibility for signing the release. Under Ohio law, he was under a duty to read the document before signing it. The Ohio Court of Appeals reversed the trial judge on the grounds that federal law (that a finding of fraud will preclude the use of a release such as the one in this case) should have been applied. The Ohio Supreme Court reversed again, and this appeal followed.

ISSUE: In adjudicating a claim arising out of federal law, may a state court properly apply state law?

HOLDING AND DECISION: (Black, J.) No. Though federal claims may be adjudicated by state courts, state laws are never controlling on the question of what the incidents of any federal right may be. Federal rights according relief to injured railroad employees could be defeated if states were permitted to have the final say as to what defenses could and could not be interposed here. It is true that Ohio normally allows the judge in an action to resolve all issues of fraud in a negligence action, and that, in itself, is a perfectly acceptable procedure. But it is well settled that the federal right to a jury trial is an essential one, which Ohio may not infringe upon. Judgment is reversed, and the judgment of the Ohio Court of Appeals is affirmed.

DISSENT: (Frankfurter, J.) Justice Frankfurter objects that requiring federal standards for the determination of fraud unconstitutionally invades the State's reserved power to maintain the common law division between law (i.e., negligence determined by a jury) and equity (fraud relieved by a judge).

EDITOR'S ANALYSIS: This case points up the general rule for the treatment of federal rights in state courts. In short, they are always governed by federal law. The Seventh Amendment right to a civil jury trial is an exclusively federal right. It is not a fundamental right incorporated in the Fourteenth Amendment and extended to the state. As such, states may properly provide that certain issues are to be determined by judges. When a federal right is involved, however, such discretion ceases. The federal standard of the Seventh Amendment must prevail.

NOTES:

NOTES

CHAPTER 5
SUPREME COURT APPELLATE JURISDICTION

QUICK REFERENCE RULES OF LAW

1. **Supreme Court Appellate Jurisdiction.** The Supreme Court may review a case only after the highest court in the state has rendered a final judgment or decree. (Radio Station WOW, Inc. v. Johnson)

2. **Freedom of the Press.** The Constitution bars a civil action against the press for publishing true information disclosed in public court documents open to public inspection. (Cox Broadcasting Corp. v. Cohn)

3. **Procedural Defaults.** A litigant's procedural defaults in state proceedings do not prevent vindication of his federal rights unless the state's insistence on compliance with its procedural rule serves a legitimate state interest. (Henry v. Mississippi)

4. **State Court Decisions.** When a state court decision fairly appears to rest primarily on federal law, or to be interwoven with the federal law, and when the adequacy and independence of any possible state law ground is not clear from the fact of the opinion, the decision whether or not the federal courts have jurisdiction to review that decision will be made by accepting as the most reasonable explanation that the state court decided the case the way it did because it believed that federal law required it to do so. (Michigan v. Long)

5

NOTES

RADIO STATION WOW, INC. v. JOHNSON

326 U.S. 120 (1945)

NATURE OF CASE: Review of decision setting aside a radio station lease and license, directing their transfer, and ordering an accounting of profits.

FACT SUMMARY: Johnson (P) contended that the Supreme Court did not have the right to review a decision by the state supreme court of Nebraska because its order that there be an accounting of profits meant that the litigation had not been concluded.

CONCISE RULE OF LAW: The Supreme Court may review a case only after the highest court in the state has rendered a final judgment or decree.

FACTS: Johnson (P) was a member of an association, the World Life Insurance Society, that owned a radio station. The Society and Radio Station WOW (D), a Nebraska Corporation that had been leasing the station, applied to the FCC to transfer the station license to WOW (D). Johnson filed suit to have the transfer set aside for fraud. Meanwhile, the FCC consented to the transfer, and the Society transfered both the station properties and the license to WOW (D). The trial court found no fraud involved in the transfer of the radio license, as Johnson (P) had alleged, and dismissed the suit. The state supreme court reversed, however, and entered judgment for Johnson (P). The court also ordered that the lease and the license be set aside and that an accounting be made of the operation of the station by Radio Station WOW (D) since it took ownership. Radio Station WOW (D) petitioned for review by the U.S. Supreme Court, but Johnson (P) argued that as long as the accounting remained to be done, the Supreme Court did not have power to intervene. The Supreme Court granted certiorari.

ISSUE: May the Supreme Court review a case only after the highest court in the state has rendered a final judgment or decree?

HOLDING AND DECISION: (Frankfurter, J.) Yes. The Supreme Court may review a case only after the highest court in the state has rendered a final judgment or decree. Litigation must be concluded in the court of first instance. Previous Supreme Court decisions, however, have ruled that an accounting does not preclude reviewability. Where, as here, a judgment has directed immediate delivery of physical property, that judgment is reviewable and is to be deemed dissociated from a provision for an accounting, even if the accounting is decreed in the same order. This is because all federal questions reviewable by the Supreme Court have been adjudicated by the state court, and an accounting could not possibly give rise to the sort of federal question that would render the state court's judgment a nonfinal order. Because it is, therefore, a final and conclusive adjudication of conflicting claims to the property used by WOW (D), the Supreme Court may review the decision below. Therefore, a Supreme Court review is permitted in this case.

EDITOR'S ANALYSIS: Concerns about administrative expediency are the principal driving force behind the requirement of finality. It is meant to prevent economic waste and delayed justice. Note that whether a litigation has been concluded so as to be sufficiently "final" to permit review is a federal question; how a state court decides the issue will not affect the Supreme Court's final analysis.

NOTES:

COX BROADCASTING CORP. v. COHN

420 U.S. 469.

NATURE OF CASE: Appeal from an action for damages for invasion of privacy.

FACT SUMMARY: Cohn (P) sued Cox Broadcasting Corp. (D) for damages for invasion of privacy under a Georgia statute which made it a misdemeanor to publish or broadcast the name or identity of a rape victim when Cox (D) reported on criminal court proceedings concerning the rape and death of Cohn's (P) daughter.

CONCISE RULE OF LAW: The Constitution bars a civil action against the press for publishing true information disclosed In public court documents open to public inspection.

FACTS: Cox (D), reporting on the court proceedings in a prosecution for rape, gave the name of the rape victim which it had learned from public records. Cohn (P), the rape victim's father, sued Cox (D) for damages for invasion of privacy under a Georgia statute which made it a misdemeanor to publish or broadcast the name or identity of a rape victim. Cox (D) claimed that its use of the name was privileged under the first and fourteenth amendments. The trial court gave summary judgment for Cohn (P). Cox (D) appealed and the Georgia Supreme Court held that the Georgia statute was inapplicable since it created no civil cause of action. Consequently, continued the court, it need not consider the issue of the constitutionality of the statute. Instead, it reversed the summary judgment holding that Cohn (P) had a common law tort claim for invasion of privacy and that the trier of fact must determine whether the public disclosure of the daughter's name actually invaded the father's zone of privacy. On rehearing the Georgia trial court relied on the misdemeanor statute as an authoritative declaration of state policy and held that the name of a rape victim is not a matter of public concern. It is then held the Georgia statute was a legitimate limitation on the right of freedom of expression contained in the first amendment. Cox (D) appealed to the United States Supreme Court invoking jurisdiction under 28 U.S.C.A. §1257 which states that the court's appellate jurisdiction with respect to state litigation can be granted only after the highest state court in which judgment could be had has rendered a final judgment or decree. The Supreme Court reversed the state court decision and held for Cox (D).

ISSUE: Does the Constitution bar a civil action against the press for publishing true information disclosed in public documents open to public inspection?

HOLDING AND DECISION: (White, J.) Yes. Although the ultimate issue was one of the constitutionality of civil actions against the press, initially this court must resolve two questions of jurisdiction arising under 28 U.S.C.A. §1257. First, was the constitutional validity of the Georgia statute drawn into issue and upheld by the Georgia Supreme Court. Second, was the decision from which this appeal has been taken a final judgment or decree. Historically, this court has appellate jurisdiction with respect to state litigation only after the highest state court in which judgment could be had has rendered a final judgment or degree. However, there are cases in which the highest state court has finally determined the federal issue present, but in which there are further proceedings in lower state courts. In these cases the Supreme Court has taken jurisdiction and such is the case at bar. Consequently, we conclude that this court has jurisdiction to review the judgment of the Georgia Supreme Court rejecting the challenge under the first and fourteenth amendments to the state law authorizing damage suits against the press for publishing the name of a rape victim whose identity is revealed in the course of a public prosecution. The Georgia Supreme Court's judgment is plainly final on the federal issue and is not subject to further review in the state courts. Although the trial court's decision as to which party might prevail is still unsettled, if the Georgia Supreme Court erroneously upheld the statute, there should be no trial at all. Moreover, delaying final decision of the first amendment claim until after trial will leave unanswered an important question of freedom of the press that could only further harm the operation of a free press. Given these factors, that the litigation could be terminated by a decision on the merits now and that a failure to decide the issue will leave the operation of the press in Georgia hampered by civil and criminal sanctions, this court finds it necessary to reach the merits. On the merits this court holds that the Constitution bars a civil action against the press for publishing true information disclosed in public court documents open to public inspection.

DISSENT: (Rehnquist, J.) I am of the opinion that the decision which is the subject of this appeal is not a final judgment as that term is used in 28 U.S.C.A. §1257. The appeal should be dismissed for want of jurisdiction. The finality requirement should not be disturbed, except in very few situations, where intermediate rulings may carry serious public consequences. The Court here, far from eschewing a constitutional holding in advance of the necessity for one, construes §1257 so that it may virtually rush out and meet the prospective constitutional litigant as he approaches our doors.

EDITOR'S ANALYSIS: As the Supreme Court enunciated in the case at bar there are times when it is not feasible to wait for a final decision. For example, there are cases in which an important right may be destroyed if a party is not able to secure immediate review. In other cases, the issue which needs review is capable of being separated from the rest of the case and prompt review will prevent the entire trial court proceeding from being held in obeyance. For these reasons, as well as others, the decisions of the Supreme Court concerning the finality issue are not altogether harmonious. Indeed the court has stated that there is not even a sure test as to what constitutes a final decision which can be applied universally to all cases.

HENRY v. MISSISSIPPI

379 U.S. 443 (1965).

NATURE OF CASE: Appeal from conviction of disturbing the peace.

FACT SUMMARY: The State of Mississippi (P) argued that Henry's (D) failure to timely object to admission of illegal evidence barred his right to a new trial and was an adequate state ground for denial of Supreme Court jurisdiction.

CONCISE RULE OF LAW: A litigant's procedural defaults in state proceedings do not prevent vindication of his federal rights unless the state's insistence on compliance with its procedural rule serves a legitimate state interest.

FACTS: The State of Mississippi (P) requires contemporaneous objection to the introduction of illegal evidence. Henry (D) was charged with disturbing the peace by indecent proposal and offensive conduct with an eighteen-year-old hitchhiker. During his trial, his attorneys failed to object to certain evidence at the time it was offered but did move for a directed verdict on illegal search and seizure grounds at the close of the State's (P) case. Henry (D) was convicted. The state supreme court initially overturned the conviction on illegal evidence grounds but then reconsidered and affirmed in light of Henry's (D) failure to comply with the contemporaneous objection rule. On appeal to the U.S. Supreme Court, the State (P) argued that the Court lacked jurisdiction under the "adequate state ground" doctrine.

ISSUE: Do a litigant's procedural defaults in state proceedings prevent vindication of his federal rights?

HOLDING AND DECISION: (Brennan, J.) No. A litigant's procedural defaults in state proceedings do not prevent vindication of his federal rights unless the state's insistence on compliance with its procedural rule serves a legitimate state interest. Ordinarily, the Supreme Court will decline to review state court judgments that rest on independent and adequate state grounds, even where those judgments also decide federal questions. But a state procedural rule cannot be permitted to bar vindication of important federal rules. It is only allowed to do so when it advances a state interest. Mississippi's contemporaneous objection rule clearly serves state interests involving timely exclusion of evidence in criminal trials. Henry's (P) directed verdict motion, however, may have satisfied those interests and thereby vitiated the state ground of decision. But even assuming that to be true, Henry's (D) attorneys may have deliberately bypassed the opportunity to make timely objections for strategic reasons, in which case Henry (D) is deemed to have forfeited his state court remedies. Therefore the conviction is vacated and remanded for a hearing on the question of whether Henry (D) knowingly waived decision of his federal claim by failure to object to the admission of illegally seized evidence at the time it was offered.

DISSENT: (Harlan, J.) The majority implies that enforcement of the State's (P) contemporaneous-objection rule was inadequate as a state ground of decision because Henry's (D) motion for a directed verdict of acquittal afforded the trial judge a satisfactory opportunity to take appropriate corrective action with reference to the allegedly inadmissible evidence by, for example, striking the tainted testimony. But there was no appropriate corrective action that could have realistically satisfied the state purposes of maximizing correct decisions and minimizing errors. Therefore, reliance on the rule was adequate to bar direct review by the Court.

EDITOR'S ANALYSIS: Several exceptions to the adequate state ground doctrine have been formulated by the Supreme Court. One states that a "novel" state procedural rule will render the doctrine inapplicable. Another suggests that the same is true for those rules that impose a heavy burden on the litigant. A third holds that the Court may review constitutional challenges raised late in the state proceedings and decided under the state court's discretionary power. Such discretionary judgments, by definition, would not implicate any vital state interest.

NOTES:

MICHIGAN v. LONG

103 S.Ct. 3469 (1983).

NATURE OF CASE: Review of a decision reversing a criminal conviction.

FACT SUMMARY: Long (D) asserted that the U.S. Supreme Court was without jurisdiction to review the Michigan Supreme Court's decision reversing his criminal conviction, his claim being that the decision below rested on an adequate and independent state ground.

CONCISE RULE OF LAW: When a state court decision fairly appears to rest primarily on federal law, or to be interwoven with the federal law, and when the adequacy and independence of any possible state law ground is not clear from the fact of the opinion, the decision whether or not the federal courts have jurisdiction to review that decision will be made by accepting as the most reasonable explanation that the state court decided the case the way it did because it believed that federal law required it to do so.

FACTS: Long (D) was convicted for possession of marijuana, but the Michigan Supreme Court reversed his conviction in an opinion that stated the search of Long's (D) vehicle was proscribed by the United States and Michigan constitutions. Michigan (P) sought review by the U.S. Supreme Court, but Long (D) insisted it had no jurisdiction to decide the case because the decision below rested on an adequate and independent state ground.

ISSUE: Will the Supreme Court review state court decisions which fairly appeal to rest primarily on federal law or to be interwoven with the federal law, including any decision in which the adequacy and independence of any possible state law ground is not clear from the face of the opinion?

HOLDING AND DECISION: (O'Connor, J.) Yes. When, as in this case, a state court decision fairly appears to rest primarily on federal law, or to be interwoven with the federal law, and when the adequacy and independence of any possible state law ground is not clear from the face of the opinion, this Court will accept as the most reasonable explanation that the state court decided the case the way it did because it believed that federal law required it to do so. Of course, if a state court decision indicates clearly and expressly that it is alternatively based on bona fide separate, adequate, and independent state grounds, this Court will not undertake to review the decision. Reversed and remanded.

CONCURRING IN PART: (Blackman, J.) I cannot join the Court in that part of its opinion that fashions a new presumption of jurisdiction over cases coming here from state courts, since I see little efficiency and an increased danger of advisory opinions in this new approach.

DISSENT: (Stevens, J.) There are four ways to resolve the question of whether the state law ground, which is clearly adequate to support the judgment of the Michigan Supreme Court's understanding of federal law. First we could ask the Michigan Supreme Court directly. Second, we could attempt to infer from all possible sources of state law what the Michigan Supreme Court meant. Third, we could presume that adequate state grounds are independent unless it clearly appears otherwise. Fourth, we could presume that adequate state grounds are not independent unless it clearly appears otherwise. While this Court has, on different occasions, employed each of the first three approaches; never until today has it even hinted at the fourth. While I find defensible its rejection of the first approach as inefficient and unduly burdensome for state courts and the second approach as an inappropriate expenditure of our resources, I cannot accept its decision to choose the fourth approach over the third. When left with a choice between two presumptions, one in favor of our taking jurisdictions and one against it, the latter presumption has always prevailed historically. I believe that in reviewing decisions of state courts, the primary role of this Court is to make sure that persons who seek to vindicate federal rights have been fairly heard. Until recently we had virtually no interest in cases of this type, but our priorities shifted during the past decade and the result has been a docket swollen with requests by states to reverse judgments that their courts have rendered in favor of their citizens.

EDITOR'S ANALYSIS: There were instances in the past in which a case was remanded to the state's highest court for purposes of clarifying whether or not its decision had been based on an independent state ground. However, in addition to the inefficiency of this method and the burden it places on state courts, another problem with this approach was illustrated in Duxon v. Duffy, 344 U.S. 143 (1952). In that instance, the U.S. Supreme Court continued the case twice for the purpose of obtaining just such a clarification from the California Supreme Court. No such clarification was ever made. The California Supreme Court informally advised the petitioner's counsel that "it doubted its jurisdiction to render such a determination." As a result, the U.S. Supreme Court had to go back and vacate the judgment of the California Supreme Court and remand the case.

NOTES:

OSBORN v. BANK OF THE UNITED STATES

22 U.S. (9 Wheat.) 738 (1824)

NATURE OF CASE: Appeal from decree ordering repayment of tax.

FACT SUMMARY: When the Bank (P) challenged the collection of a tax by the State Auditor of Ohio (D), Ohio (D) claimed that the federal courts lacked jurisdiction.

CONCISE RULE OF LAW: Congress may constitutionally authorize the federal courts to assume total jurisdiction over a case arising under federal law even though other nonfederal questions of law or fact might also be involved.

FACTS: The State of Ohio (D) passed a law levying a tax on all branches of the Bank of the United States (P) located within the state. Shortly thereafter, the case of McCulloch v. Maryland was decided, holding a similar tax void. The Bank (P) then sued to enjoin Ohio (D) from enforcing its tax law. Hoping to collect the tax before the injunction could be issued, Osborn (D), the Ohio State Auditor, went to the Bank (P) and physically seized a portion of its assets. The federal court entered a decree ordering Ohio (D) to repay the amount seized, plus interest, to the Bank (P). Ohio (D) appealed, partly on the ground that the federal courts did not properly have jurisdiction over the action, since the basic issues involved state rather than federal law.

ISSUE: Is an act of Congress authorizing federal courts to assume total jurisdiction over an action arising under federal law but also involving questions of nonfederal law constitutionally valid?

HOLDING AND DECISION: (Marshall, C.J.) Yes. Initially, it must be stated that the act of Congress that established the Bank (P) clearly authorizes the Bank (P) to sue in federal court. Thus, it is only the constitutionality of that provision which must be decided. Article III of the Constitution establishes the Supreme Court and defines cases in which it shall exercise original jurisdiction. In all other federal cases, it has appellate jurisdiction only. However, this is not to say that inferior federal courts cannot exercise original jurisdiction in other federal cases as Ohio (D) attempts to argue. Thus, if this case is found to arise under federal law, the circuit court may assume jurisdiction. The Bank (P) is totally a creature of federal statute. It cannot acquire a right, make a contract or bring a suit not ultimately authorized by federal law. As such, all of its actions must be seen as arising under federal law. Nonetheless, Ohio (D) contends that only those precise issues involving federal law may be presented to the federal courts. Other issues in the suit involving principles of state law may not be heard by the federal courts. This is not the law. If the powers of the federal court were to be so restricted, they would be rendered nearly powerless since virtually no case will be wholly devoid of nonfederal questions of law or fact. Instead, the Constitution must be read as permitting Congress to authorize the federal courts to exercise total jurisdiction over an action arising under federal law even though other nonfederal questions of law or fact might also be involved. Affirmed.

DISSENT: (Johnson, J.) Although it is true, as the majority states, that a federal court may assume jurisdiction over all questions involved in an action which principally arises under federal law, this principle does not permit federal jurisdiction in the action at hand. In this case, no federal question has arisen. Thus, federal jurisdiction is premature and not called for.

DISSENT: (Johnson, J.) Neither the Constitution nor the Congress intended to permit the vesting of an unlimited right of action in the Bank of the United States (P) in cases in which the privilege is exclusively personal or in any case merely on the ground that a federal question might possibly be raised.

EDITOR'S ANALYSIS: In the Pacific Railroad Removal Cases, 115 U.S. 1 (1885), the Court held that any case involving a corporation chartered by an act of Congress fell within the ambit of "suits arising under the laws of the United States," thus allowing federal courts to assume jurisdiction. This ruling was severely limited by the subsequent enactment of 28 U.S.C.A. § 1349, which provides for jurisdiction in the federal courts on the ground of federal incorporation only when, in addition, the United States is the owner of more than 50% of the capital stock of the corporation.

NOTES:

NOTES

CHAPTER 6
FEDERAL QUESTION JURISDICTION

QUICK REFERENCE RULES OF LAW

1. **Nonfederal Questions of Law or Fact.** Congress may constitutionally authorize the federal courts to assume total jurisdiction over a case arising under federal law even though other nonfederal questions of law or fact might also be involved. (Osborn v. Bank of the United States)

2. **Labor Disputes.** The federal courts may fashion a federal substantive law regarding labor contracts in labor disputes involving federal rights. (Textile Workers Union of America v. Lincoln Mills of Alabama)

3. **Patent Suits.** A suit for damages caused to one's business by a threat to sue for patent infringement is not a suit under the patent laws, and therefore may not be maintained in federal court. (American Well Works Co. v. Layne & Bowler Co.)

4. **Stating a Claim.** A federal district court has jurisdiction where it appears from the plaintiff's bill that the right to relief rests upon the construction or application of the Constitution or law of the United States and that such a claim rests upon a reasonable foundation. (Smith v. Kansas City Title & Trust Co.)

5. **Stating a Claim.** When Congress has determined that there should be no private federal cause of action for violation of a particular federal statute, a complaint alleging a violation of that statute as an element of a state cause of action does not state a claim "arising under the Constitution, laws, or treaties of the United States." (Merrell Dow Pharmaceuticals Inc. v. Thompson)

6. **Federal Question.** A federal court may not exercise jurisdiction over a case merely because an anticipated defense or the response thereto will involve a federal question. (Louisville and Nashville Railroad Co. v. Mottley)

7. **Federal Question.** The existence of a federal question must be established by the plaintiff's own claim, and may not depend upon an anticipated defense or the response to a defense. (Skelly Oil Co. v. Phillips Petroleum Co.)

8. **Federal Question.** Congress has given the lower federal courts jurisdiction to hear, originally or by removal to a state court, only those cases in which a well-pleaded complaint establishes either that federal law creates the cause of action or that the plaintiff's right to relief necessarily depends on resolution of a substantial question of federal law. (Franchise Tax Board of the State of California v. Construction Laborers Vacation Trust for Southern California)

NOTES

TEXTILE WORKERS UNION v. LINCOLN MILLS

353 U.S. 448 (1957).

NATURE OF CASE: Petition for writ of certiorari in a suit to compel arbitration of a labor-management grievance.

FACT SUMMARY: Following the making of a "collective-bargaining agreement" with the Textile Workers Union (P) providing for no strikes or work stoppages, Lincoln Mills (D) failed to comply with that part of the agreement which provided for arbitration.

CONCISE RULE OF LAW: The federal courts may fashion a federal substantive law regarding labor contracts in labor disputes involving federal rights.

FACTS: A collective-bargaining agreement was entered into between the Textile Workers Union (P) and Lincoln Mills (D). The agreement provided that there would be no strikes or work stoppages and that either party could submit grievances to arbitration. However, Lincoln Mills (D) subsequently refused when the Union (P) requested arbitration to resolve several grievances concerning work loads and work assignments. Therefore, the Union (P) brought this suit to compel arbitration. The district court concluded that it had jurisdiction and ordered Lincoln Mills (D) to comply with the arbitration provisions. However, the court of appeals reversed, holding that, although there was jurisdiction, the district court had no authority founded in either federal or state law to grant relief. The Supreme Court granted the Union's (P) petition for writ of certiorari.

ISSUE: May the federal courts fashion a federal substantive law regarding labor contracts in those labor disputes involving federal rights?

HOLDING AND DECISION: (Douglas, J.) Yes. The federal courts may fashion a federal substantive law regarding labor contracts in those labor disputes involving federal rights. Section 301 (a) of the Labor Management Relations Act of 1947 provides that employer-union contract violation suits in an industry affecting commerce may be brought in any district court having jurisdiction. Section 301(b) supplements 301(a) to make it possible for a labor organization representing employees in an industry affecting commerce to sue and be sued as an entity in the federal courts. According to one view, 301(a) is not a source of substantive law but merely a source of the court's jurisdiction in labor controversies affecting commerce. However, we hold, along with the large majority of courts, that 301(a) authorizes the federal courts to fashion a body of federal law for the enforcement of collective-bargaining agreements and includes within that federal law specific performance of promises to arbitrate grievances under collective-bargaining agreements. This holding is based on the legislative history of § 301 which shows that Congress regarded the agreement to arbitrate as a quid pro quo of a no-strike agreement. Were this court not to enforce the sanctions behind these agreements to arbitrate, we would render the Act powerless to accomplish its purposes. The substantive law that the courts are to apply in suits under § 301(a) is to be fashioned from our national labor laws. This presents no constitutional problem. Article III, § 2 extends the judicial power to cases "arising under the laws of the United States." The power of Congress to regulate these labor-management controversies under the Commerce Clause is plain. A case or controversy under § 301(a) is therefore within the judicial power as defined in Article III. Reversed.

DISSENT: (Frankfurter, J.) Section 301 of the Taft-Hartley Act should not be construed as a mandate to the federal courts to fashion a whole body of federal law for collective bargaining. Nothing pertaining to § 301 suggests vesting the federal courts with sweeping power under the Commerce Clause comparable to that vested in the federal courts under the bankruptcy power.

EDITOR'S ANALYSIS: The above case is one of the three most celebrated instances of assumption of law-making power by the federal courts based on jurisdictional grants. The second is the power to create federal admiralty law implied from Article III's grant of admiralty jurisdiction. This implication is the same, not only of judge-made law, but also of Congress' power to legislate on admiralty matters. The third is the law governing litigation between the states: law-making power is implied from the jurisdictional grant over interstate controversies and justified by the inappropriateness of using any one state's law.

NOTES:

AMERICAN WELL WORKS CO. v. LAYNE & BOWLER CO.

241 U.S. 257 (1916).

NATURE OF CASE: Suit to recover damages for injuries to a business.

FACT SUMMARY: American (P) manufactured and sold a pump. Layne & Bowler (D) alleged that the pump infringed its patent, threatening to sue American (P) and all purchasers of the product.

CONCISE RULE OF LAW: A suit for damages caused to one's business by a threat to sue for patent infringement is not a suit under the patent laws, and therefore may not be maintained in federal court.

FACTS: American Well Works Co. (P) produced and began selling a certain type of pump, allegedly the best on the market. Layne & Bowler (D) claimed that the pump resembled parts of the pump sold by Layne & Bowler (D), and threatened to sue both American (P) and its customers. In fact, suits were actually commenced against some of American's (P) customers. A suit was then filed in state court in which American (P) sought damages for the harm caused to its business by the litigation, threats, and accusations undertaken by Layne & Bowler (D). The action was later removed to federal district court, whereupon American (P) moved to have the case remanded to the state court. The federal tribunal ruled that, since the cause of action had arisen under the patent laws of the United States, the state court lacked jurisdiction over the case in the first place and the federal court was therefore not entitled to exercise removal jurisdiction. On appeal, it was contended that the cause of action was not based on the patent laws and thus presented no federal question.

ISSUE: May a federal court exercise jurisdiction over a suit alleging damage to a business as a result of a threat to sue for patent infringement?

HOLDING AND DECISION: (Holmes, J.) No. A suit for damages caused to one's business by a threat to sue for patent infringement is not a suit under the patent laws and therefore may not be maintained in federal court. Such an action presents no federal question because it is not the patent, but the damage caused to the business, which is the basis for the cause of action. Whether or not the type of interference is actionable is purely a matter of state law. Therefore, this suit is not one to which federal jurisdiction attaches.

DISSENT: (McKenna, J.) The case clearly involves a controversy arising under the patent laws, and thus presents a federal question.

EDITOR'S ANALYSIS: The authority of the federal courts to exercise jurisdiction over patent matters is expressly conferred by 28 U.S.C. § 1338. However, federal decisional law has made it clear that the state courts have jurisdiction over many actions involving aspects of patent law. The various decisions apportioning jurisdiction over patent matters between state and federal courts are not entirely reconcilable, but they obviously demonstrate the fact that a litigant in a patent case has considerable latitude in deciding whether to proceed in a state or a federal forum.

NOTES:

SMITH v. KANSAS CITY TITLE & TRUST CO.

255 U.S. 180 (1921).

NATURE OF CASE: Shareholders' suit to enjoin company from purchasing certain bonds.

FACT SUMMARY: Kansas City Title & Trust Co. (D) was permitted by its charter to invest in legal securities. When Trust Co. (D) sought to purchase federal farm loan bonds, authorized by an act of Congress and declared by that act to be a lawful investment for fiduciary and trust funds, Smith (P), a shareholder in Trust Co. (D), sought to enjoin the investment on the ground that the act in question was unconstitutional.

CONCISE RULE OF LAW: A federal district court has jurisdiction where it appears from the plaintiff's bill that the right to relief rests upon the construction or application of the Constitution or law of the United States and that such a claim rests upon a reasonable foundation.

FACTS: The Federal Farm Loan Act of 1916 authorized the establishment of Federal Land Banks and Joint-Stock Land Banks and provided that farm loan bonds issued by such banks were lawful investments for all fiduciaries and trust funds as well as acceptable security for all public deposits. Smith (P), a shareholder in Trust Co. (D), filed a bill in district court to enjoin such an investment by Trust Co. (D), arguing that the Act authorizing the issuance of such bonds was unconstitutional, and seeking such a declaration. Two of the banks established under the Act were permitted to intervene as party defendants. Trust Co. (D) demurred to Smith's (P) bill and, after a hearing, the district court dismissed the bill. Smith (P) appealed to the Supreme Court.

ISSUE: When a controversy concerns the validity of an act of Congress that is directly drawn in question by the pleadings, does a district court have jurisdiction?

HOLDING AND DECISION: (Day, J.) Yes. A federal district court has jurisdiction where it appears from the plaintiff's bill that the right to relief rests upon the construction or application of the Constitution or law of the United States and that such a claim rests upon a reasonable foundation. Where diversity of citizenship is lacking, as in the instant case, the United States Judicial Code § 24 gives the district court jurisdiction if the cause of action set forth arises under the Constitution or laws of the United States. Such a cause of action arises when the case, for its decision, depends upon a construction of either the Constitution or a law of the United States. In the instant case, Smith (P) attacks the proposed investment by Trust Co. (D) on the sole ground that the act of Congress authorizing the bonds and declaring them to be a lawful investment for trust funds is unconstitutional. Trust Co. (D) maintains that the act, and therefore the bonds, are valid. Therefore, the district court had jurisdiction under the averments of the bill. The judgment of the district court dismissing the bill must be affirmed on the merits, however.

DISSENT: (Holmes, J.) The district court did not have jurisdiction because the cause of action does not arise under the Constitution or laws of the United States. On the contrary, Smith's (P) right of action is based on Missouri law only. It is Missouri which granted the corporation its charter and defines the scope of corporate duty toward the shareholder. A suit cannot be said to arise out of any other law than that which creates the cause of action, because it must be the suit itself and not merely a question in the suit that arises under the Constitution or law of the United States. Since there is no jurisdiction, the merits should not have been considered.

EDITOR'S ANALYSIS: Holmes' dissent indicates the ambiguity in the phrase "arising under" and proposes a conservative interpretation that would limit the number of cases which would meet federal jurisdictional requirements. Holmes suggests that if the plaintiff's right of action or right to bring suit is based upon state law, the mere fact that a federal law is challenged does not mean that there is a cause of action "arising under" such law. But the right to bring suit may not be the actual source of the cause faction. Many commentators, including the American Law Institute, have thus rejected any proposed statutory definition of the term "arising under," preferring to leave untouched the traditional language and its interpretation by the courts.

NOTES:

MERRELL DOW PHARMACEUTICALS, INC. v. THOMPSON

478 U.S. 804 (1986).

NATURE OF CASE: Action for damages for drug-related birth defects.

FACT SUMMARY: Merrell Dow Pharmaceuticals, Inc. (D) successfully moved to have the Thompsons' (P) suit for damages for drug-related birth defects removed to federal court despite the Thompsons' (P) contention that the federal court lacked subject-matter jurisdiction.

CONCISE RULE OF LAW: When Congress has determined that there should be no private federal cause of action for violation of a particular federal statute, a complaint alleging a violation of that statute as an element of a state cause of action does not state a claim "arising under the Constitution, laws, or treaties of the United States."

FACTS: The Supreme Court granted certiorari to review an appellate decision reversing the district court's determination that federal jurisdiction existed with respect to suits brought in state court by the Thompsons (P) and the MacTavishes (P) to recover damages for birth defects caused by the ingestion of the drug Benedectin. The complaints alleged the drug was misbranded in violation of the Federal Food, Drug, and Cosmetic Act and that this created a rebuttable presumption of negligence. They provided no federal private cause of action for its violation.

ISSUE: Does federal jurisdiction exist when a complaint alleges a violation of a federal statute as an element of a state cause of action but the federal statute does not provide for a private federal cause of action for its violation?

HOLDING AND DECISION: (Stevens, J.) No. A complaint alleging a violation of a federal statute as an element of a state cause of action, when Congress has determined that there should be no private federal cause of action for the violation, does not state a claim "arising under the Constitution, laws, or treaties of the United States." The congressional determination that there should be no federal remedy for the violation of this federal statute is tantamount to a congressional conclusion that the presence of a claimed violation of the statute as an element of a state cause of action is insufficiently "substantial" to confer federal question jurisdiction. Affirmed.

DISSENT: (Brennan, J.) There is federal jurisdiction where the plaintiff's right to relief "necessarily depends" upon resolution of a federal question. The decision not to provide a federal remedy does not automatically mean that federal jurisdiction is lacking.

EDITOR'S ANALYSIS: The majority opinion embraces an approach initially taken as commentators attempted to explain seemingly irreconcilable results in cases dealing with the issue of federal-question jurisdiction. Commentators had suggested the decisions were best understood as an evaluation of the nature of the federal interest at stake in each case, with a significant interest being required for jurisdiction to attach.

NOTES:

LOUISVILLE AND NASHVILLE RAILROAD v. MOTTLEY

211 U.S. 149 (1908).

NATURE OF CASE: Suit to compel specific performance of a contract.

FACT SUMMARY: The Mottleys (P) were injured in a collision of Louisville & Nashville (D) trains. In exchange for lifetime passes, the Mottleys (P) released the railroad (D) from all claims for damages.

CONCISE RULE OF LAW: A federal court may not exercise jurisdiction over a case merely because an anticipated defense or the response thereto will involve a federal question.

FACTS: In September of 1871, the Mottleys (P) were injured when the Louisville & Nashville R.R. (D) train in which they were traveling collided with another train owned by the Railroad (D). The Mottleys (P) agreed to release the Railroad (D) from all potential damage claims in exchange for free passes, renewable annually. The Railroad (D) sent the passes each year until 1907 when Congress enacted a law which precluded common carriers from granting free transportation. The Mottleys (P), who were citizens of Kentucky, sued the Railroad (D), also a Kentucky citizen, in federal court. Their suit prayed for specific performance of the Railroad's (D) agreement to provide lifetime passes and asserted that the act of Congress did not prevent the issuance of passes under the circumstances. They argued alternatively, that if construed as prohibiting their issuance, the statute was unconstitutional because it deprived the Mottleys (P) of their property without due process of law. The trial court granted the relief sought, but the Railroad (D) appealed directly to the Supreme Court.

ISSUE: May federal jurisdiction be exercised in a case if the only federal question involved will arise in connection with an anticipated defense or the response thereto?

HOLDING AND DECISION: (Moody, J.) No. A federal court may not exercise jurisdiction over a case merely because an anticipated defense or the response thereto will involve a federal question. There is no basis for diversity jurisdiction, and the federal law which the Mottleys (P) challenge need not be considered except as a defense offered by the Railroad (D). Since the issue of federal law was not raised by the complaint itself, federal jurisdiction did not attach. Thus, although the Railroad (D) offered no objection, the court below had no basis for exercising jurisdiction over this case and should have dismissed the Mottleys' (P) complaint.

EDITOR'S ANALYSIS: Federal courts may exercise jurisdiction over cases with issues arising under the Constitution, laws or treaties of the United States. This jurisdiction derives from the first paragraph of Article III, § 2, of the Constitution. However, the rule of Louisville & Nashville R.R. v. Mottley, that the federal question involved in a case must arise from the plaintiff's complaint, unaided by potential defenses, has been recognized as authoritative. The Mottley rule seems reasonable and desirable since a plaintiff could almost always imagine a plausible defense by his adversary that would involve an issue of federal law.

NOTES:

SKELLY OIL CO. v. PHILLIPS PETROLEUM CO.

339 U.S. 667 (1950).

NATURE OF CASE: Suit seeking a declaratory judgment.

FACT SUMMARY: Skelly Oil Company's (D) contract to sell gas to Phillips Petroleum Co. (P) was contingent upon the Michigan-Wisconsin Pipe Line Company's (P) receipt of a "certificate of public convenience and necessity."

CONCISE RULE OF LAW: The existence of a federal question must be established by the plaintiff's own claim, and may not depend upon an anticipated defense or the response to a defense.

FACTS: The Michigan-Wisconsin Pipe Line Company (P), anxious to construct a pipe line to carry natural gas from Texas to Michigan and Wisconsin, applied to the Federal Power Commission (FPC) for a certificate of public convenience and necessity. To obtain the certificate, Michigan-Wisconsin (P) had to prove that it had access to adequate reserves of gas. Michigan-Wisconsin (P) therefore contracted with Phillips (P), who agreed to make gas available from the Hugoton Gas Field, a field located in the southwestern United States. Phillips (P) contracted with Skelly (D), Stanolind Oil and Gas Company (D) and Magnolia Petroleum Company (D). Phillips (P) agreed to purchase gas from these Companies (D), but the contracts with each company (D) provided that, should Michigan-Wisconsin (P) fail to obtain its certificate of public convenience and necessity by October 1, 1946, each gas company (D) would have the right after December 1, 1946 but before the issuance of a certificate to terminate its contract with Phillips (P). On November 30, 1946, the FPC issued a certificate of public convenience and necessity to Michigan-Wisconsin (P). Several burdensome conditions were attached to the issuance of that certificate, some of which were to be incorporated into a supplemental order. Michigan-Wisconsin (P) was given fifteen days from the issuance of the supplemental order to accept or refuse the certificate. The FPC's decision was made public on December 2, 1946, and, on that date, Skelly (D), Stanolind (D) and Magnolia (D) each gave notice terminating their contracts with Phillips (P). All three companies were sued in federal district court by Michigan-Wisconsin (P) and Phillips (P), both of which sought relief under the Federal Declaratory Judgment Act. They claimed that, inasmuch as a certificate had been issued to Michigan-Wisconsin (P) before Skelly (D), Stanolind (D) and Magnolia (D) had sent termination notices, the contracts with the three companies (D) should be declared to be in force. Michigan-Wisconsin (P) was ultimately dropped from the case by the district court, but motions to dismiss the complaint for want of jurisdiction were denied. The district court ruled that the contested contracts were still in effect, and the appellate court affirmed. In seeking redress from the Supreme Court, Skelly (D), Stanolind (D) and Magnolia (D) renewed their claim that the district court had lacked jurisdiction in the first place because the case did not present a federal question.

ISSUE: May the existence of a federal question be established by reference to an anticipated defense or the response to that defense?

HOLDING AND DECISION: (Frankfurter, J.) No. The existence of a federal question must be established by the plaintiff's own claim and may not depend upon an anticipated defense or response to a defense. Any federal claim that Phillips (P) could possibly have raised had it not invoked the Declaratory Judgment Act could have arisen only as a defense by one of the other companies (D), or in response to such a defense. The action was brought pursuant to the Act only because Phillips (P) sought a predicate for federal jurisdiction. But the Declaratory Judgment Act does not expand the jurisdiction of federal courts. It merely empowers them to grant declaratory relief in cases over which they were already entitled to exercise jurisdiction. Had Phillips (P) not invoked the Act, it could have sued for either damages or specific performance, but neither of these remedies would have required the consideration of questions of federal law. If federal jurisdiction could be based on an anticipated defense, the docket of the federal tribunals would become dangerously overloaded. Therefore, the claims against Skelly (D) and Stanolind (D) should have been dismissed. However, since Magnolia (D) is a citizen of a different state than Phillips (P), the suit against Magnolia (D) was cognizable in the federal courts because of diversity jurisdiction. Nevertheless, the judgment against Magnolia (D) should be reversed. The lower court erred in assuming that because a certificate was issued to Michigan-Wisconsin (P) under the language of The Natural Gas Act , a certificate was issued within the meaning of the contract between Phillips (P) and Magnolia (D). The words in the statute may have a different meaning than the parties intended them to have in the contract. Therefore, the judgments against Skelly (D) and Stanolind (D) should be reversed and the claims against them dismissed, while the case against Magnolia (D) should be remanded for further proceedings.

CONCURRENCE AND DISSENT: (Vinson, C.J.) The judgments against Skelly (D) and Stanolind (D) should, as the majority decides, be dismissed. But the judgment against Magnolia (D) should be affirmed, because Michigan-Wisconsin (P) clearly was issued a certificate within the meaning of the Phillips (P)-Magnolia (D) contract.

EDITOR'S ANALYSIS: A litigant desiring to predicate federal jurisdiction upon the fact that his claim presents a question arising under the Constitution or laws of the United States must meet the burden of establishing that his complaint actually involves such an issue. If, at any stage of the proceedings, the federal court concludes that no federal question is presented and there is no other basis for invoking its jurisdiction, that court may properly dismiss the case. Statutory grants of federal jurisdiction are strictly construed in order to prevent the ready entry into federal court which has, in recent years, swelled the caseloads of many federal tribunals.

FRANCHISE TAX BOARD OF CALIFORNIA v. CONSTRUCTION LABORERS VACATION TRUST FOR SOUTHERN CALIFORNIA

463 U.S. 1 (1983).

NATURE OF CASE: Action seeking damages and declaratory relief.

FACT SUMMARY: The Franchise Tax Board (P) insisted that its suit against CLVT (D) should not have been removed from state court to federal district court.

CONCISE RULE OF LAW: Congress has given the lower federal courts jurisdiction to hear, originally or by removal to a state court, only those cases in which a well-pleaded complaint establishes either that federal law creates the cause of action or that the plaintiff's right to relief necessarily depends on resolution of a substantial question of federal law.

FACTS: The Franchise Tax Board (P) sought to collect unpaid state income taxes by levying on funds held in trust for the taxpayers under a vacation benefit plan, CLVT (D), covered by the federal Employment Retirement Income Security Act (ERISA). The complaint it filed in state court asked both for recovery of such monies and for a declaratory judgment to the effect that CLVT (D) was obligated to honor such levies by the Board (P) despite CLVT's (D) assertion that ERISA preempts state law and precludes honoring such levies. CLVT (D) succeeded in having the case removed to federal district court, which the Board (P) argued was improper.

ISSUE: In order for a case to be removable to federal court, must it be one in which a well-pleaded complaint establishes that federal law creates the cause of action or that the plaintiff's right to relief necessarily depends on resolution of a substantial question of federal law?

HOLDING AND DECISION: (Brennan, J.) Yes. Congress has given the lower federal courts jurisdiction to hear, originally or by removal from a state court, only those case in which a well-pleaded complaint establishes either that federal law creates the cause of action or that plaintiff's right to relief necessarily depends on resolution of a substantial question of federal law. The suit at issue here is neither a creature of ERISA itself nor a suit of which the federal courts will take jurisdiction because it turns on a question of federal law. If, but for the availability of the declaratory judgment procedure (either state or federal) the federal claim would arise only as a defense to a state-created action, as in this case, jurisdiction is lacking. It is clear from the foregoing that removal was improper in this case. Judgment vacated.

EDITOR'S ANALYSIS: The outcome would have been different had the court found that the preemptive force of ERISA was so powerful as to displace entirely any state cause of action. Prior case law made it clear that if a federal cause of action completely preempts a state cause of action, any complaint that comes within the scope of the federal cause of action necessarily "arises under" federal law.

NOTES:

NOTES

CHAPTER 7
FEDERAL COMMON LAW

QUICK REFERENCE RULES OF LAW

1. **Commercial Paper.** The rights and duties of the United States on commercial paper which it issues are governed by federal rather than local law. (Clearfield Trust Co. v. United States)

2. **Competing Federal and Private Liens.** State law is the appropriate federal rule of decision for establishing the relative priority of competing federal and private liens. (United States v. Kimbell Foods, Inc.)

3. **Liability for Design Defects in Military Equipment.** Liability for design defects in military equipment cannot be imposed when the equipment conforms to specifications approved by the government. (Boyle v. United Technologies Corporation)

4. **The Act of State Doctrine.** The act of state doctrine, which precludes inquiry into the validity of the official acts of a foreign government committed within its own territory, is applicable even if international law has been violated. (Banco Nacional de Cuba v. Sabbatino)

5. **Violation of the Fourth Amendment.** Violation of the Fourth Amendment by a federal agent acting under color of his authority may give rise to a private cause of action for damages. (Bivens v. Six Unknown Named Agents of Federal Bureau of Narcotics)

6. **Conflicting Policy Considerations.** When Congress has constructed an elaborate remedial system with careful attention to conflicting policy considerations, the courts should not create new alternative remedies. (Bush v. Lucas)

7. **Implied Causes of Action.** A federal cause of action will be implied if such is part of the overall legislative purpose of the federal statute in question. (Thompson v. Thompson)

8. **Maritime Contracts.** A maritime contract may be governed by state law if the application of state law does not disturb the uniformity of maritime law. (Kossick v. United Fruit Co.)

NOTES

CLEARFIELD TRUST CO. v. U.S.

318 U.S. 363.

NATURE OF CASE: Appeal from an action to recover money on a check.

FACT SUMMARY: The United States (P) brought suit in the federal district court against the Clearfield Trust Co. (D) seeking reimbursement of forged a Works Progress Administration check which Clearfield (D) cashed and expressly guaranteed by prior endorsements.

CONCISE RULE OF LAW: The rights and duties of the United States on commercial paper which it issues are governed by federal rather than local law.

FACTS: A check drawn on the Treasurer of the United States and made payable to Claire Barner was cashed by an unknown party who endorsed the check in the name of Barner and transferred it to J.C. Penney Co. J.C. Penney Co. endorsed the check over to Clearfield Trust Co. (D). Clearfield (D) collected on the check from the United States (P), expressly guaranteeing it by prior endorsements. Barner then informed the WPA that he had not received the check. Over a year later, Clearfield (D) received notice that the United States (P) was seeking reimbursement. Suit was instituted over another year later by the United States (P) in the federal district court based on the express guarantee of prior endorsements made by Clearfield. The district court dismissed the complaint on the ground that the rights of the parties were to be determined by the law of Pennsylvania, the place of the transaction, and that, since the United States (P) unreasonably delayed in giving notice of the forgery to Clearfield (D), it was barred from recovery. The court of appeals reversed.

ISSUE: Are the rights and duties of the United States on commercial paper which it issues governed by federal rather than local law?

HOLDING AND DECISION: (Douglas, J.) Yes. When the United States disburses its funds or pays its debts, it is exercising a constitutional function. This check was issued for services performed under the Federal Emergency Relief Act of 1935. The authority to issue the check had its origin in the Constitution and the statutes of the United States and was in no way dependent on the laws of Pennsylvania or any other state. In absence of an applicable act of Congress, it is for the federal courts to fashion the governing rule of law according to their own standards. Although in our choice of the applicable federal rule we have occasionally selected state law, the reasons which make state law at times the appropriate federal rule are inappropriate in the instant case. The issuance of commercial paper by the United States is on a vast scale, commonly occurring in several states. Therefore, the application of state law would subject the rights and duties of the United States to exceptional uncertainty. The desirability of a uniform rule is plain. As to the issue of prompt notice, this court holds that lack of such notice will be a defense. If it is shown that the drawee, on learning of the forgery, did not give prompt notice of it and that damage resulted, recovery by the drawee is barred. But the damage must be established and not left to conjecture as was done in the case at bar. No such damage has been shown by Clearfield who can still recover from J. C. Penney Co. Consequently, the decision of the court of appeals is affirmed.

EDITOR'S ANALYSIS: Justice Jackson, in the case of D'Oench, Duhme & Co., stated that "a federal court sitting in a non-diversity case does not sit as a local tribunal. In some cases it may see fit for special reasons to give the law of a particular state highly persuasive or even controlling effect, but in the last analysis its decision turns upon the law of the United States. Federal law is no judicial chameleon changing complexion to match that of each state wherein lawsuits happen to be commenced because of the accidents of service of process and of the application of the venue statutes."

NOTES:

UNITED STATES v. KIMBELL FOODS, INC.

440 U.S. 715 (1979).

NATURE OF CASE: Review of judgment declaring a new federal rule to determine relative priority of security interests in lien foreclosure action.

FACT SUMMARY: The federal government (D) persuaded the court of appeals to fashion a uniform national rule to determine the priority of a private lien and a Small Business Association lien.

CONCISE RULE OF LAW: State law is the appropriate federal rule of decision for establishing the relative priority of competing federal and private liens.

FACTS: Kimbell Foods (P) secured a loan to O.K. Super Markets by placing a lien on its equipment and merchandise. O.K. Super Markets then obtained another loan guaranteed by the Small Business Association (SBA). O.K. later defaulted on this debt. Shortly thereafter, Kimbell Foods (P) sued O.K. to recover its inventory debt. O.K. sold its equipment and inventory and placed the proceeds in escrow. After Kimbell Foods (P) received a judgment against O.K., it then sued the federal government (D), claiming that its security interest in the escrow fund was superior to the SBA's. The district court held for the government (D), but the appeals court reversed. It fashioned a new federal rule for determining which lien was first in time based on which lien qualified as first perfected. The federal government (D) appealed, and the Supreme Court granted certiorari.

ISSUE: Is state law the appropriate federal rule for establishing the relative priority of competing federal and private liens?

HOLDING AND DECISION: (Marshall, J.) Yes. State law is the appropriate federal rule for establishing the relative priority of competing federal and private liens. Federal law governs all questions involving the rights of the United States arising under nationwide federal programs. Therefore, the priority of liens stemming from federal lending programs must be determined by referring to federal law. However, that does not mean that courts must resort to a uniform federal rule. A nationwide federal rule is only necessary when a nationally uniform body of law is required or when state law would frustrate specific objectives of a federal program. On the other hand, if application of a federal rule would disrupt existing commercial relationships predicated on state law, then adoption of state law should be considered. In this case, nationwide standards are not necessary to protect the federal interest. Moreover, incorporating state law to determine priority rights would not hinder administration of the SBA loan programs. Finally, businessmen depend on the stability of state commercial law when they are structuring financial transactions. Therefore, although governed by federal law, the relative priority of liens arising from government lending programs is to be determined under nondiscriminatory state laws. Reversed.

EDITOR'S ANALYSIS: The Supreme Court subsequently applied its Kimbell Foods test to determine whether state or federal law should govern a boundary dispute on the shores of a river separating private property owners and Native Americans living on a reservation. See Wilson v. Omaha Indian Tribe, 442 U.S. 653 (1979). As in the Kimbell Foods case, the Court ultimately refused to develop a general body of federal common law. Instead, it chose to apply state real property law, reasoning that states had a substantial interest in employing their own laws to resolve land disputes — laws upon which landowners relied when purchasing real property.

NOTES:

BOYLE v. UNITED TECHNOLOGIES CORP.
487 U.S. 500 (1988).

NATURE OF CASE: Appeal of award of damages for wrongful death.

FACT SUMMARY: The Sikorsky Division (D) of United Technologies sought immunity from tort actions relating to the helicopters it built for the United States Navy.

CONCISE RULE OF LAW: Liability for design defects in military equipment cannot be imposed when the equipment conforms to specifications approved by the government.

FACTS: The Sikorsky Division (D) of United Technologies built the CH-53D helicopter for the United States military. Boyle's (P) son, a Marine helicopter copilot, was killed when the CH-53D helicopter he was flying crashed into the ocean during a training exercise; he survived the impact but drowned when he was unable to escape the helicopter. Boyle (P) brought suit against Sikorsky (D), contending that it had defectively repaired a device in the automatic flight control system and had defectively designed the emergency escape system. A jury awarded Boyle (P) $725,000. The court of appeals reversed, ruling that Sikorsky (D) could not be held liable for defective design since it was entitled to the "military contractor defense." Boyle (P) appealed, and certiorari was granted.

ISSUE: May a military contractor be held liable for defective design relating to a product which was built for the U.S. government and conforms to government specifications?

HOLDING AND DECISION: (Scalia, J.) No. Liability for design defects in military equipment cannot be imposed when the equipment was built for the U.S. government and conforms to specifications approved by the government. The procurement of equipment by the U.S. government is an area of uniquely federal interest. Where uniquely federal interests are involved, the federal common law preempts state law to the extent that there is a conflict. A state-imposed duty of care is in direct conflict with a government contract which specifies a certain design. Therefore, federal law displaces state tort law with regard to the procurement of equipment by the federal government. The Federal Tort Claims Act exempts discretionary functions of the government from liability. The selection of the appropriate design for military equipment is a discretionary function; thus, federal law provides immunity to military contractors. The scope of this immunity covers equipment which conforms to specifications which have been approved by the United States. The supplier must also warn the government about the dangers of use since there would be incentive to withhold information because of the immunity. Sikorsky (D) supplied the CH-53D helicopters to the U.S. military after the design had been approved by the Navy. Therefore, Sikorsky (D) was entitled to the immunity provided by federal law, and Boyle's (P) award was properly reversed. Affirmed.

DISSENT: (Brennan, J.) State laws should not be displaced by federal law except where Congress has explicitly decided to supersede them or in a few narrow circumstances. Military contractors have long lobbied unsuccessfully for immunity in Congress. Furthermore, the category of "uniquely federal interests" has never before been extended to the conduct of nongovernment employees such as government contractors.

DISSENT: (Stevens, J.) Where an entirely new doctrine such as the military contractor defense is created, the proper decision maker should be Congress because only the legislature has the proper means to balance the conflicting interests which are involved.

EDITOR'S ANALYSIS: Since the decision, Congress extended the Federal Tort Claims Act immunity to cover all conduct by federal officials within the scope of their employment, whether discretionary or not. In Trevino v. General Dynamics Corp., 865 F.2d 1474 (5th Cir. 1989), which was decided subsequent to Boyle, the court ruled that a government employee's signature on each page of a contractor's design drawings wasn't necessarily the approval required by Boyle.

NOTES:

BANCO NACIONAL de CUBA v. SABBATINO

376 U.S. 398 (1964).

NATURE OF CASE: Appeal from summary judgment for the defense in action to recover proceeds from conversion of bills of lading.

FACT SUMMARY: Banco Nacional de Cuba (P) contended that the act of state doctrine precluded a federal court from invalidating a Cuban expropriation decree affecting a shipment of sugar purchased by Farr, Whitlock (D).

CONCISE RULE OF LAW: The act of state doctrine, which precludes inquiry into the validity of the official acts of a foreign government committed within its own territory, is applicable even if international law has been violated.

FACTS: Banco Nacional de Cuba (P), an instrumentality of the Cuban government, claimed the right to the proceeds of a shipment of sugar expropriated by the president of Cuba. It sued Farr, Whitlock (D), the purchaser of the sugar, and temporary receiver Sabbatino (D) for conversion of the bills of lading. Farr, Whitlock (D) argued that the expropriation of the sugar was in violation of international law and thus did not convey good title to Banco Nacional (P). The district court agreed and entered summary judgment against Banco Nacional (P). The court of appeals affirmed, and Banco Nacional (P) appealed, arguing that Cuba's actions must be respected as the act of a sovereign state pursuant to the act of state doctrine.

ISSUE: Is the act of state doctrine applicable even if international law has been violated?

HOLDING AND DECISION: (Harlan, J.) Yes. The act of state doctrine, which precludes inquiry into the validity of the official acts of a foreign government committed within its own territory, is applicable even if international law has been violated. The doctrine is binding on both federal and state courts. It is not found in the text of the Constitution but instead is a reflection of the proper distribution of functions between the judicial and political branches of the government. The validity of nationalization and expropriation of the property of aliens may be questionable, but it is not the sort of international policy issue in which the courts should intervene. Reversed and remanded.

EDITOR'S ANALYSIS: The seminal case involving the act of state doctrine is Underhill v. Hernandez, 168 U.S. 250, in which Chief Justice Fuller stated: "Every sovereign State is bound to respect the independence of every other sovereign State, and the courts of one country will not sit in judgment on the acts of the government of another done within its own territory. Redress of grievances by reason of such acts must be obtained through the means open to be availed of by sovereign powers as between themselves." Justice Fuller was applying a doctrine that took root in England as early as 1674.

NOTES:

BIVENS v. SIX UNKNOWN NAMED AGENTS OF FEDERAL BUREAU OF NARCOTICS

403 U.S. 388 (1971).

NATURE OF CASE: Appeal from dismissal of claim for damages for an unlawful arrest.

FACT SUMMARY: Federal agents (D) argued that Bivens (P) could obtain money damages for invasion of his right to privacy following his arrest only by an action in tort, under state law, in the state courts.

CONCISE RULE OF LAW: Violation of the Fourth Amendment by a federal agent acting under color of his authority may give rise to a private cause of action for damages.

FACTS: Bivens (P) was arrested by six agents (D) of the Federal Bureau of Narcotics who entered his apartment and manacled him in front of his wife and children. Alleging that the arrest and search were done without a warrant, Bivens (P) sued the agents (D) for $15,000 each. The district court dismissed the complaint on the ground that it failed to state a cause of action. The appellate court affirmed. Bivens (P) appealed, and the Supreme Court granted certiorari.

ISSUE: May violation of the Fourth Amendment by a federal agent acting under color of his authority give rise to a private cause of action for damages?

HOLDING AND DECISION: (Brennan, J.) Yes. Violation of the Fourth Amendment by a federal agent acting under color of his authority may give rise to a private cause of action for damages. The Fourth Amendment guarantees the absolute right to be free from unreasonable searches and seizures carried out by virtue of federal authority. When a federally protected right is violated, federal courts may use any available remedy. Bivens's (P) complaint states a cause of action under the Fourth Amendment. Therefore, he is entitled to recover money damages for any injuries he suffered as a result of the agents' (D) violation of the Amendment. Reversed and remanded.

CONCURRENCE: (Harlan, J.) The judiciary has a particular responsibility to assure the vindication of constitutional interests, by compensatory relief if appropriate, even without express congressional authorization.

DISSENT: (Burger, J.) The Constitution vests legislative power in Congress; the doctrine of separation of powers dictates that Congress, not the courts, should create a damage remedy not provided for by the Constitution.

DISSENT: (Black, J.) Neither Congress nor the State of New York has legislation creating a remedy against federal officials who violate the Fourth Amendment. Even if courts had the power to create such a remedy, the growing number of frivolous suits would counsel against it.

EDITOR'S ANALYSIS: Note that Congress created a federal cause of action against state officials acting under color of state law when it enacted 42 U.S.C § 1983. It has never created such a cause of action against federal officials. Subsequent to the Bivens decision, the Supreme Court enunciated two situations in which a Bivens cause of action may be defeated: (1) when defendants demonstrate special factors counseling hesitation, and (2) when defendants show that Congress has provided an alternative remedy explicitly declared to be a substitute for recovery directly under the Constitution.

NOTES:

BUSH v. LUCAS

462 U.S. 367 (1983).

NATURE OF CASE: Review of summary judgment rejecting claim for damages for defamation and violation of constitutional rights.

FACT SUMMARY: Bush (P) contended that his First Amendment rights were violated when he was demoted for publicly criticizing NASA, his employer, and that civil service remedies did not fully compensate him for the harm he suffered.

CONCISE RULE OF LAW: When Congress has constructed an elaborate remedial system with careful attention to conflicting policy considerations, the courts should not create new alternative remedies.

FACTS: Bush (P), a federal civil servant employed by NASA, claimed he was the victim of a retaliatory demotion by his supervisor, Lucas (D). The Civil Service Commission's Appeals Review Board agreed, and recommended that Bush (P) be restored to his former position and given back pay. Both recommendations were accepted. While his administrative appeal was pending, however, Bush (P) also filed suit against Lucas (D) in Alabama state court, seeking to recover damages for defamation and violation of his constitutional rights. Lucas (D) removed the action to federal district court and moved for summary judgment. The court granted his motion, concluding that Bush (P) had no cause of action for damages for retaliatory discharge under the First Amendment in view of the available remedies under the Civil Service Commission regulations. Bush (P) appealed.

ISSUE: When Congress has constructed an elaborate remedial system with careful attention to conflicting policy considerations, should the courts create new remedies?

HOLDING AND DECISION: (Stevens, J.) No. When Congress has constructed an elaborate remedial system with careful attention to conflicting policy considerations, the courts should not create new alternative remedies. The federal courts have the power to grant relief not expressly authorized by Congress. However, they must first consider any special factors or reasons why Congress alone should prescribe what remedies should be available. In this case, a federal employee whose First Amendment rights has been violated by a supervisor is presently protected by an elaborate, comprehensive scheme that provides meaningful remedies. Furthermore, if all managers faced the risk of personal liability for decisions, they would be deterred from imposing discipline in future cases. Congress is in the best position to decide whether the creation of a new substantive legal liability would serve the public interest. Affirmed.

CONCURRENCE: (Marshall, J.) A Bivens remedy is unnecessary in this case because Congress has already created a comprehensive scheme as effective as an individual damages remedy, which is specifically designed to provide full compensation to civil servants like Bush (P).

EDITOR'S ANALYSIS: Bush's (P) action against Lucas (D) was predicated on the Supreme Court decision in Bivens v. Six Unknown Fed. Narcotics Agents, 403 U.S. 388 (1971), in which the Court held that the Constitution itself supports a private cause of action for damages against a federal official. The Bivens Court warned, however, that prior to authorizing a new kind of federal litigation, courts must consider any "special factors counseling hesitation in the absence of affirmative action by Congress." Bush (P) sought a Bivens remedy because the administrative procedure created by Congress did not permit recovery for loss due to emotional distress and mental anguish.

NOTES:

THOMPSON v. THOMPSON

108 Sup.Ct. 513, 98 L.Ed.2d 512 (1988).

NATURE OF CASE: Appeal from dismissal of petition for child custody.

FACT SUMMARY: Mr. Thompson (P) contended that a federal cause of action was implied in the Parental Kidnapping Prevention Act to allow federal courts to determine competing claims to the effectiveness of sister state custody determinations.

CONCISE RULE OF LAW: A federal cause of action will be implied if such is part of the overall legislative purpose of the federal statute in question.

FACTS: The Thompsons divorced in California, that state's court ordering joint custody of their minor child. Mrs. Thompson (D) then received sole custody so that she could move to Louisiana to pursue employment. The California court retained jurisdiction to consider modifying custody permanently. Mrs. Thompson (D) gained permanent sole custody from a Louisiana court. Mr. Thompson (P) brought suit in federal court seeking a determination of the validity of the California custody order. The district court held the Parental Kidnapping Prevention Act, governing the situation, did not imply a federal cause of action to determine controversy under the Act. Mr. Thompson (P) appealed the dismissal, and the court of appeals affirmed. The Supreme Court granted certiorari.

ISSUE: Will a federal cause of action be implied if such is part of the overall legislative scheme announced by the statute in question?

HOLDING AND DECISION: (Marshall, J.) Yes. A federal cause of action will be implied only if such is part of the purpose of the legislative scheme announced by the statute in question. The Act was enacted to trigger the Full Faith and Credit Clause and to apply it to state court custody decrees. By providing a mechanism in the statute to determine what state would have primary jurisdiction, the statute sought to avoid problems created by competing state judgments. To recognize a federal cause of action would in effect emasculate the statute and render it useless. Because it would not promote the statutory scheme, it was not implied in the statute. Affirmed.

CONCURRENCE: (O'Connor, J.) The Act does not create a federal cause of action.

CONCURRENCE: (Scalia, J.) The implied cause of action must rest upon Congressional intent which unmistakenly creates the right without actually articulating it. It is a much narrower standard than that identified in the Court's decision.

EDITOR'S ANALYSIS: Federal jurisdiction has always been extremely limited and encompasses only cases arising under federal law or those involving diversity jurisdiction. Strict compliance is necessary. Thus, the Court is very reluctant to expand jurisdiction by implying federal causes of action where such is not articulated in the statute.

KOSSICK v. UNITED FRUIT CO.

365 U.S. 731 (1961).

NATURE OF CASE: Review of dismissal of action for damages for breach of an oral agreement.

FACT SUMMARY: When seaman Kossick's (P) breach of contract claim against shipowner United Fruit Co. (D) was barred by the New York Statute of Frauds, he argued that maritime law should apply instead.

CONCISE RULE OF LAW: A maritime contract may be governed by state law if the application of state law does not disturb the uniformity of maritime law.

FACTS: United Fruit Co. (D) employed Kossick (P) as a chief steward on one of its vessels. All shipowners had a duty to provide maintenance and care for their employees. When Kossick (P) developed a thyroid condition, he reluctantly agreed to be treated at a United States Public Health Service Hospital, but only on the condition that United Fruit (D) pay to correct any improper or inadequate treatment he might receive there. Kossick (P) claimed that he did, in fact, receive improper treatment at the hospital. He sued United Fruit (D) for $250,000 in damages. The district court dismissed on the ground that United Fruit's (D) oral agreement to assume liability was void under New York's Statute of Frauds. The appeals court agreed. Kossick (P) appealed, arguing that oral contracts are regarded as valid by maritime law. The Supreme Court granted certiorari.

ISSUE: May a maritime contract be governed by state law if the application of state law does not disturb the uniformity of maritime law?

HOLDING AND DECISION: (Harlan, J.) Yes. A maritime contract may be governed by state law if the application of state law does not disturb the uniformity of maritime law. The agreement here qualifies as a maritime contract. Nevertheless, if it is sufficiently "local" in nature, its validity should be judged by state law. This contract was not peculiarly a matter of state or local concern. Since the application of state law would invalidate the contract, it cannot be compared to those cases rejecting the application of maritime law where state law actually supplemented the remedies available in admiralty law. Therefore, the New York Statute of Frauds should not have been applied to bar proof of the agreement alleged in Kossick's (P) complaint. Reversed.

DISSENT: (Frankfurter, J.) The duty to observe the "uniformity of maritime law" is a loose, ill-starred legal doctrine that should not prevent the Statute of Frauds from governing an essentially local transaction like this one.

DISSENT: (Whittaker, J.) The oral contract claimed by Kossick (P) was not a maritime contract, but a New York contract barred by its statute of frauds.

EDITOR'S ANALYSIS: The majority distinguished its holding from the conclusion reached by the Court in Wilburn Boat Co. v. Fireman's Ins. Co., 348 U.S. 310 (1955). Wilburn involved an insurance dispute arising from a fire aboard a houseboat situated on a small artificial lake between Texas and Oklahoma. The Court chose to apply state law to that case since there was no applicable federal maritime law to govern the matter. The Court also reasoned that the regulation of insurance has traditionally been a state function.

NOTES:

CHAPTER 8
DIVERSITY JURISDICTION

QUICK REFERENCE RULES OF LAW

1. **Diversity of Citizenship.** In a case brought in federal court based on diversity of citizenship, there must be complete diversity between the parties. (Strawbridge v. Curtiss)

2. **A Corporation's Principal Place of Business.** A corporation's principal place of business is a question of fact that does not follow any single inflexible test dependent solely upon the situs of the nerve center or upon the situs of activities of the corporation. (J.A. Olson Co. v. City of Winona)

3. **Federal Diversity Jurisdiction.** An unincorporated association cannot be considered a "citizen" for purposes of establishing federal diversity jurisdiction. (United Steelworkers of America, AFL-CIO v. R.H. Bouligny, Inc.)

4. **Requirements to Establish Domicile.** Residence in fact and the intention of making the place of residence one's home are essential elements of domicile. (Stine v. Moore)

5. **The Domestic Relations Exception to Diversity Jurisdiction.** The domestic relations exception to diversity jurisdiction encompasses only cases involving the issuance of a divorce, alimony, or child custody decree. (Ankenbrandt v. Richards)

6. **Judicial Code.** Under the Judicial Code, where an assignment of a cause of action is improper or collusively made to invoke federal diversity jurisdiction, the district court may not have cognizance of the suit. (Kramer v. Caribbean Mills, Inc.)

NOTES

STRAWBRIDGE v. CURTISS

7 U.S. 267, 3 Cranch 267 (1806).

NATURE OF CASE: Appeal from a dismissal for want of jurisdiction.

FACT SUMMARY: Since the plaintiff and all of the defendants, except Curtiss (D), were citizens of Massachusetts, the Circuit Court of Massachusetts dismissed the complaint for want of diversity jurisdiction.

CONCISE RULE OF LAW: In a case brought in federal court based on diversity of citizenship, there must be complete diversity between the parties.

FACTS: Strawbridge (P) and the defendants were citizens of Massachusetts, except Curtiss (D) who was averred to be a citizen of Vermont. The circuit court dismissed the suit for want of diversity jurisdiction. Strawbridge (P) appealed.

ISSUE: In a case brought in federal court based on diversity of citizenship, must there be complete diversity between the parties?

HOLDING AND DECISION: (Marshall, C.J.) Yes. In this act, Congress defined diversity jurisdiction as "where an alien is a party, or the suit is between a citizen of a state where the suit is brought, and a citizen of another state." This means that each distinct interest should be represented by persons, all of whom are entitled to sue or may be sued in the federal courts. Since there is not complete diversity between the parties the district court correctly dismissed the case.

EDITOR'S ANALYSIS: It has been stated that Justice Marshall regretted the decision in Strawbridge. However, except for the interpleader cases, the rule of complete diversity enunciated in this case has been consistently upheld. In the interpleader cases, the statute requires only that "two or more adverse claimants, of diverse citizenship" be parties. That is, this so-called minimal diversity requires only that one plaintiff and one defendant be from different states.

NOTES:

J.A. OLSON CO. v. CITY OF WINONA

818 F.2d 401 (5th Cir. 1987).

NATURE OF CASE: Appeal from dismissal of complaint for lack of diversity of citizenship.

FACT SUMMARY: Attempting to refute J.A. Olson's (P) claim of diversity jurisdiction, the City of Winona (D), Mississippi, argued that J.A. Olson's (P) principal place of business was in Winona (D), where its manufacturing and storage facilities were located, not in Chicago, where its primary financial and management decisions were made.

CONCISE RULE OF LAW: A corporation's principal place of business is a question of fact that does not follow any single inflexible test dependent solely upon the situs of the nerve center or upon the situs of activities of the corporation.

FACT SUMMARY: J.A. Olson (P) was an Illinois corporation with its sole manufacturing plant in Winona (D), Mississippi. The Winona (D) office processed Olson's (P) orders, maintained bookkeeping records and sales showrooms, and made significant management decisions. The corporate headquarters were in Chicago, where Olson's (P) corporate records and major bank accounts were maintained. J.A. Olson (P) sued the City of Winona (D), basing jurisdiction on diversity of citizenship. Winona (D) moved to dismiss for lack of jurisdiction because Olson's (P) principal place of business was Mississippi. The district court agreed and dismissed Olson's (P) complaint. Olson (P) appealed.

ISSUE: Is a corporation's principal place of business a fact question that follows no single inflexible test dependent solely upon the situs of the nerve center or upon the situs of activities of the corporation?

HOLDING AND DECISION: (Jolly, J.) Yes. A corporation's principal place of business is a question of fact that does not follow any single inflexible test dependent solely upon the situs of the nerve center or upon the situs of activities of the corporation. The "total activity" test determines the principal place of business of a corporation. The place of activity and the nerve center of a corporation are two of the components of the "total activity" test. When considering a corporation engaged in far-flung and varied activities that are carried on in different states, the sole nerve center or "brain" of that corporation is more significant in determining principal place of business. However, when a corporation has its sole operation in one state and its executive offices in another, the place of activity is regarded as more significant. In this case, Olson's (P) sole maufacturing activity is in Winona (D). It is where (1) the vast majority of Olson's (P) employees are located, (2) Olson (P) is most visible, (3) its products are manufactured, and (4) its corporate purpose if fulfilled. Although decisions made in Chicago are important, they cannot outweigh the significance of the activities conducted in Winona (D). Therefore, Winona (D) is Olson's (P) principal place of business. Dismissal affirmed.

EDITOR'S ANALYSIS: The purpose of diversity jurisdiction is to provide a federal forum for out-of-state litigants where they will be free from prejudice in favor of a local litigant. Before 1958, a corporation was deemed a citizen only of its state of incorporation. In 1958, the scope of diversity jurisdiction was narrowed when Congress amended 28 U.S.C. § 1332(a) to make a corporation a citizen not only of the state in which it was incorporated but also of the state of its principal place of business.

NOTES:

UNITED STEELWORKERS v. R. H. BOULIGNY, INC.

382 U.S. 145 (1965).

NATURE OF CASE: Suit seeking damages for defamation.

FACT SUMMARY: Bouligny (P) sued the Steelworkers (D) in state court, alleging defamation. The union (D), claiming diversity of citizenship, sought to have the action removed to federal court.

CONCISE RULE OF LAW: An unincorporated association cannot be considered a "citizen" for purposes of establishing federal diversity jurisdiction.

FACTS: R. H. Bouligny, Inc. (P), a North Carolina corporation, sued the United Steelworkers (D) in state court. The action accused the Steelworkers (D), an unincorporated association which claimed Pennsylvania as its principal place of business, of defamation. The Steelworkers (D), alleging that the case involved a federal question and that there was diversity of citizenship between the parties, succeeded in having the suit removed to federal district court. However, the Fourth Circuit Court of Appeals, finding no federal question and concluding that an unincorporated association was not a citizen for purposes of demonstrating diversity of citizenship, ordered the case remanded to the state courts. The United States Supreme Court then granted certiorari.

ISSUE: Does an unincorporated association qualify as a " citizen" for purposes of proving federal diversity jurisdiction?

HOLDING AND DECISION: (Fortas, J.) No. An unincorporated association cannot be considered a "citizen" for purposes of establishing federal diversity jurisdiction. This is the rule which has been recognized since 1889, when the seminal case of Chapman v. Barney was decided. The district court judge alertly observed a trend toward treating corporations and unincorporated associations identically. And, there seems to be little reason to recognize a distinction between the two forms of organization, since they are so similar in structure and operation. Many associations would benefit from the privilege of being able to establish federal diversity jurisdiction. In fact, labor unions, which to some people represent a threat to the economy and to the racial mores of a community, are especially deserving of the protection from local bias which federal courts lack. Unfortunately, however, to permit an unincorporated association to prove itself a citizen might create insurmountable problems, including that of determining which of the many states in which it operates should be designated the state of the association's citizenship. Therefore, despite the merits of the Steelworkers' (D) arguments, it should be left to Congress to modify the rule which presently precludes an unincorporated association from establishing its citizenship.

EDITOR'S ANALYSIS: Contemporary commentators have voiced support for the suggestion that unincorporated associations be permitted to establish citizenship. The American Law Institute has proposed that any association eligible to sue or be sued be deemed a citizen of the state in which it has its principal place of business. Such a rule would place associations and corporations on a more equal footing.

NOTES:

STINE v. MOORE

213 F.2d 446 (5th Cir. 1979).

NOTES:

NATURE OF CASE: Appeal from dismissal of breach of contract action.

FACT SUMMARY: Stine (P), a citizen of Louisiana, contended that Moore (D) was a citizen of Texas for diversity purposes, but Moore (D) argued that he had recently moved to Louisiana with the intention of remaining there permanently.

CONCISE RULE OF LAW: Residence in fact and the intention of making the place of residence one's home are essential elements of domicile.

FACTS: In his diversity suit against Moore (D), Louisiana citizen Stine (P) claimed that Moore (D) was a citizen and resident of Texas. Moore (D) paid poll taxes and voted in Texas, paid Texas income taxes, and maintained a residence and post office box there. But Moore (D) argued that he had changed his domicile in 1947, when he moved from Texas to Louisiana with the intention of making Louisiana his home. The district court agreed and dismissed the complaint. Stine (P) appealed.

ISSUE: Are residence in fact and the intention of making the place of residence one's home essential elements of domicile?

HOLDING AND DECISION: (Holmes, J.) Yes. Residence in fact and the intention of making the place of residence one's home are essential elements of domicile. Domicile is the place where an individual has his true, fixed, and permanent home, to which he intends to return. Words may be evidence of someone's intention to establish his domicile at a particular place of residence, but the actual fact of residence and the intention to remain are the controlling factors in ascertaining domicile. Any person may make a bona fide change of domicile at any time, and Moore (D) had both the residence in fact and the purpose to make Louisiana his home in 1947. Affirmed.

EDITOR'S ANALYSIS: Because domicile is an individual's true, fixed home, a citizen may have only one domicile at any time, regardless of multiple residences or different businesses. Evidentiary factors to be considered when determining domicile include: current residence, place of employment, location of bank accounts, memberships, civic participation, and car registration. Coerced or involuntary changes of residence — e.g., by incarceration — will not affect an established domicile.

ANKENBRANDT v. RICHARDS

___ U.S. ___, 112 S. Ct. 2206 (1992).

NATURE OF CASE: Appeal from dismissal of tort action seeking monetary damages for sexual and physical abuse.

FACT SUMMARY: The district court dismissed Ankenbrant's (P) lawsuit against Richards (D), her former husband, for alleged sexual and physical abuse of their children, concluding that it fell within the domestic relations exception to diversity jurisdiction.

CONCISE RULE OF LAW: The domestic relations exception to diversity jurisdiction encompasses only cases involving the issuance of a divorce, alimony, or child custody decree.

FACTS: Ankenbrant (P) brought a tort suit against her former husband, Richards (D), alleging that Richards (D) sexually and physically abused their children. The lawsuit was brought in federal court pursuant to diversity jurisdiction. The district court dismissed the complaint on the ground that it lacked jurisdiction over the case because it fell within the "domestic relations" exception to diversity jurisdiction. Ankenbrant (P) appealed, and the Supreme Court granted certiorari.

ISSUE: Does the domestic relations exception to diversity jurisdiction encompass only cases involving the issuance of a divorce, alimony, or child custody decree?

HOLDING AND DECISION: (White, J.) Yes. The domestic relations exception to diversity jurisdiction encompasses only cases involving the issuance of a divorce, alimony, or child custody decree. This rule, although based on dicta from the 1859 case of Barber v. Barber, 21 How. 582, has been recognized for nearly 150 years. However, the Barber case did not intend to strip the federal courts of authority to hear cases arising from the domestic relations of persons unless they seek the granting or modification of a divorce or alimony decree. Subsequent cases expanded the exception to include decrees in child custody cases. The lawsuit in this case does not seek any of these three decrees; it alleges that Richards (D) committed torts against his children. Federal subject-matter jurisdiction is proper. Reversed.

EDITOR'S ANALYSIS: The rationale behind the domestic relations exception is that family relations are unique because they involve matters of state policy and concern. Furthermore, they may involve retention of jurisdiction by the court and compliance monitoring. In addition, state courts are closely associated with the types of local government organization dedicated to handling conflicts arising from divorce and child custody decrees.

NOTES:

KRAMER v. CARIBBEAN MILLS, INC.

394 U.S. 823 (1969).

NATURE OF CASE: Certiorari to resolve whether a district court had proper diversity jurisdiction under the Judicial Code.

FACT SUMMARY: After receiving an assignment of a contract cause of action for nominal consideration from a Panamanian corporation, Kramer (P) sued Caribbean Mills, Inc. (D), a Haitian corporation in a district court in diversity jurisdiction. The district court judge denied a motion to dismiss for improper jurisdiction by Caribbean Mills, Inc. (D) and found for Kramer (P).

CONCISE RULE OF LAW: Under the Judicial Code, where an assignment of a cause of action is improper or collusively made to invoke federal diversity jurisdiction, the district court may not have cognizance of the suit.

FACTS: Kramer (P) received an assignment of a contract cause of action from a Panamanian Corporation against Caribbean Mills, Inc. (D), a Haitian corporation. Kramer (P) paid one dollar for the assignment and promised to pay back 95% of any net recovery. Kramer (P) sued Caribbean Mills, Inc. (D) in district court invoking diversity jurisdiction, and Caribbean Mills, Inc. (D) moved to dismiss for improper and collusively created jurisdiction under the Judicial Code. Motion denied. Judgment for Kramer (P). Reversed on appeal. Certiorari granted.

ISSUE: Does the Judicial Code permit the creation of diversity jurisdiction through the collusive assignment of a cause of action?

HOLDING AND DECISION: (Harlan, J.) No. Under the Judicial Code, where an assignment of a cause of action is collusively or otherwise improperly made merely to invoke federal diversity jurisdiction, a district court may not take cognizance of the suit. One purpose of the revised Judicial Code is to prevent the manufacture of federal jurisdiction in diversity by assignment. Kramer (P) admitted that the assignment was motivated by a desire to invoke diversity jurisdiction. The mere fact that the assignment was valid under state law and involved a foreign national corporation is irrelevant. Judgment of the court of appeals is affirmed.

EDITOR'S ANALYSIS: Federal courts jealously guard their limited jurisdiction. Because of this, devices used to create federal diversity jurisdiction are frowned upon. It is elementary, of course, that Fed. R. Civ. P. 8a requires that federal diversity jurisdiction be pleaded in any complaint seeking it. This case points up an extension of the policy of carefulness in determining the existence of true diversity — the rule that diversity cannot be created by collusion. Most commonly, this rule is applied where an administrator, guardian, or trustee is appointed solely for the purpose of creating diversity. Note, however, that while this is true, most writers agree that there is no reason why diversity could not be defeated by a collusive joinder since the statute which prevents the former, 28 USC 1359, does not apply to the latter situation.

CHAPTER 9
SUPPLEMENTAL JURISDICTION

QUICK REFERENCE RULES

1. **Pendent Jurisdiction.** Under pendent jurisdiction, federal courts may decide state issues which are closely related to the federal issues being litigated. (United Mine Workers of America v. Gibbs)

2. **Equity Rule 30.** Two classes of counterclaims are provided for under Equity Rule 30: (a) one "arising out of the transaction which is the subject matter of the suit," which must be pleaded, and (b) another "which might be the subject of an independent suit in equity" and which may be brought forward at the option of the defendant. (Moore v. New York Cotton Exchange)

3. **Cognizable Claims.** Federal courts cannot assert jurisdiction over any party not named in a claim that is independently cognizable by the federal court. (Finley v. United States)

NOTES

UNITED MINE WORKERS OF AMERICA v. GIBBS

383 U.S. 715 (1966).

NATURE OF CASE: Action to recover damages for violation of § 303 of the Labor Management Relations Act and for interference with a business interest.

FACT SUMMARY: Gibbs (P) lost his job as superintendent of a coal mining company because of alleged unlawful influence of United Mine Workers (D).

CONCISE RULE OF LAW: Under pendent jurisdiction, federal courts may decide state issues which are closely related to the federal issues being litigated.

FACTS: There was a dispute between United Mine Workers (D) and the Southern Labor Union over who should represent the coal miners in that area. Tennessee Consolidated Coal Company closed down a mine where over 100 men belonging to United Mine Workers (D) were employed. Later, Grundy Company, a wholly owned subsidiary of Tennessee Consolidated Coal Company hired Gibbs (P) to open a new mine using members of the Southern Labor Union. Gibbs (P) was also given a contract to haul the mine's coal to the nearest railroad loading point. Members of Local 5881 of the United Mine Workers (D) forcibly prevented the opening of the mine. Gibbs (P) lost his job and never entered into performance of his haulage contract. He soon began to lose other trucking contracts and mine leases he held in the area. Gibbs (P) claims this was a result of a concerted union plan against him. He filed suit in the United States District Court for the Eastern District of Tennessee for violation of § 303 of the Labor Management Relations Act and a state law claim based on the doctrine of pendent jurisdiction that there was an unlawful conspiracy and boycott aimed at him to interfere with his contract of employment and haulage. The jury's verdict was that the United Mine Workers (D) had violated both § 303 and the state law. On motion, the trial court set aside the award of damages for the haulage contracts and entered a verdict for United Mine Workers (D) on the issue of violation of § 303, the federal claim. The award as to the state claim was sustained. The court of appeals affirmed.

ISSUE: Can federal courts decide state issues that are closely related to the federal issues being litigated?

HOLDING AND DECISION: (Brennan, J.) Yes. When there are both state and federal claims involved in the same set of facts and the claims are such that the plaintiff would ordinarily be expected to try them all in one judicial proceeding, the federal court has the power to hear both the state and the federal claims. The federal claims must have substance sufficient to confer subject matter jurisdiction on the court. This is the doctrine of pendent jurisdiction. The court isn't required to exercise this power in every case. It has consistently been recognized that pendent jurisdiction is a doctrine of discretion, not plaintiff's right. The Court should look at judicial economy, convenience and fairness to litigants in deciding whether to exercise jurisdiction over the state claims. If the factual relationship between the state and federal claims is so close that they ought to be litigated at the same trial, the Court ought to grant pendent jurisdiction in order to save an extra trial. If the issues are so complicated that they are confusing to the jury, then the Court probably should dismiss the state claims. The issue of whether pendent jurisdiction has been properly assumed is one that remains open throughout the litigation. If, before the trial, the federal claim is dismissed, then the state claim should also be dismissed. If it appears that a state claim constitutes the real body of a case, then it may fairly be dismissed. The Court went on to hold that the plaintiff could not recover damages for conspiracy under the state claim. To that effect, the judgment was reversed.

EDITOR'S ANALYSIS: This case helped clarify the law that had been established by the case of Hurn v. Oursler, 289 U.S. 238. This case set the rule for determining if a federal court could hear the state claim. If a case had two distinct grounds in support of a single cause of action, one of which presents a federal question, then the court could hear the state claim. But if a case had two separate and distinct causes of action and only one was a federal question, then the court could not hear the state claim. Now the state and federal claims can state separate causes of action as long as they are factually closely related.

NOTES:

MOORE v. NEW YORK COTTON EXCHANGE

270 U.S. 593 (1926).

NATURE OF CASE: Appeal from an order of the U.S. Court of Appeals making permanent a district court injunction based on a counterclaim in a contract dispute.

FACT SUMMARY: The Circuit Court of Appeals sustained the order of the district court refusing an interlocutory injunction to Moore (P) and granting one for the New York Cotton Exchange (NYCE) (D) on a counterclaim, and Moore (P) appealed.

CONCISE RULE OF LAW: Two classes of counterclaims are provided for under Equity Rule 30: (a) one "arising out of the transaction which is the subject matter of the suit," which must be pleaded, and (b) another "which might be the subject of an independent suit in equity" and which may be brought forward at the option of the defendant.

FACTS: Moore (P) sued New York Cotton Exchange (NYCE) (D), based on the Sherman Law and questioning the validity of a contract between NYCE (D) and Western Union, which provided for cotton exchange quotations to be distributed only to selected persons. NYCE (D) counterclaimed, and both parties moved for interlocutory injunctions. The district court denied Moore's (P) motion and granted that of appellees. Upon appeal, both orders were affirmed by the court of appeals. By stipulation of the parties, the court of appeals remanded the cause with instructions to the district court to enter a final decree dismissing the bill and making permanent the injunction granted appellees. Moore (P) appealed, claiming the NYCE (D) counterclaim did not arise out of any transaction which was the subject matter of the suit. The counterclaim, on which the injunction was based, alleged that certain other persons were purloining the cotton exchange quotations, and sought to enjoin such unauthorized use.

ISSUE: Under Equity Rule 30, are there two classes of counterclaims?

HOLDING AND DECISION: (Sutherland, J.) Yes. Under Equity Rule 30, there are two classes of counterclaims: (a) one " arising out of the 'transaction' which is the subject matter of the suit," which must be pleaded, and (b) another "which might be the subject of an independent suit in equity" and which may be brought forward at the option of the defendant. "Transaction" is a word of flexible meaning. It may comprehend a series of many occurrences, depending not so much upon immediateness of their connection as upon their logical relationship. Here, the refusal to furnish the quotations is one of the links in the chain which constitutes the transaction upon which Moore (D) bases his cause of action. It is an important part of the transaction constituting the subject-matter of the counterclaim. It is the circumstance without which neither party would have found it necessary to seek relief. That the counterclaim embraces additional allegations does not matter. Affirmed.

EDITOR'S ANALYSIS: As with other joinder rules, the modern theory of counterclaims in federal court is to allow unlimited joinder at the pleading stage, with power in the court to order the separate trial of particular issues if more convenient or desirable. The modern rules of federal civil procedure recognize two distinct classes of counterclaims. If the defendant's claim falls under Rule 13(a), it is termed a "compulsory counterclaim" and must be asserted as such or be forever barred. Other claims defendant has against plaintiff that do not fit the definition of 13(a) are "permissive counterclaims" under 13(b), which permits a defendant to assert such a claim, but does not require him to do so. It has been said that the test is whether the issues of fact and law embraced in the counterclaim are largely the same. See Nachtman v. Crucible Steel Co. of America, C.A. 3d, 1948, 165 F.2d 997, 999.

NOTES:

FINLEY v. UNITED STATES
490 U.S. 545 (1989).

NATURE OF CASE: Appeal from reversal of grant of motion to include pendent claims in an action.

FACT SUMMARY: Finley (P) appealed from a decision reversing the district court's decision granting his motion to amend his federal complaint asserting claims against original state court defendants for which no independent basis for federal jurisdiction existed, contending the Federal Tort Claims Act (FTCA) permitted the assertion of pendent jurisdiction over the defendants.

CONCISE RULE OF LAW: Federal courts cannot assert jurisdiction over any party not named in a claim that is independently cognizable by the federal court.

FACTS: Finley (P) originally brought suit against the San Diego Gas and Electric Co. (Company) (D) and the city of San Diego (City) (D) in state court for the deaths of her husband and two of her children in an airplane crash. Her claim against the City (D) was based upon the negligent maintenance of the runway lights. She later learned that the FAA (D) was responsible for maintenance of the lights and brought suit against the FAA (D) under the Federal Tort Claims Act (FTCA). Almost a year later, she moved to amend her federal complaint to include claims against the Company (D) and City (D), for which no independent basis for federal jurisdiction existed. The district court granted the motion, but the court of appeals reversed, rejecting the assertion of "pendent-party" jurisdiction under the FTCA. Finley (P) appealed, and the Supreme Court granted certiorari.

ISSUE: Can federal courts assert jurisdiction over any party not named in a claim that is independently cognizable by the federal court?

HOLDING AND DECISION: (Scalia, J.) No. Federal courts cannot assert jurisdiction over any party not named in a claim that is independently cognizable by the federal court. This case, which involves so-called "pendent-party" jurisdiction, is fundamentally different from cases involving pendent claim jurisdiction, which allows the assertion of jurisdiction over nonfederal claims between parties litigating other matters properly before the court. Federal courts have limited jurisdiction as delineated by Congress, and careful attention must be paid to relevant statutory language when considering "pendent-party" claims. Here, there was no independent basis for federal jurisdiction against the Company (D) or the City (D), and the mere factual similarity of the claims did not justify an extension of ancillary jurisdiction. The language of the FTCA does not confer a grant of jurisdiction over these nonfederal claims, nor is such a grant of jurisdiction mandated by changes in the jurisdictional grant of the FTCA. Although some judicial economy is sacrificed, the language of the FTCA, which Congress is free to change, mandates the present result. Affirmed.

DISSENT: (Stevens, J.) This case is unquestionably an "Article III" case that the district court had both the constitutional and statutory power to hear under the FTCA. Congressional intent to exclude such pendent-party claims is neither express nor implicit in the language of the FTCA.

EDITOR'S ANALYSIS: As of December 1, 1990, express statutory authority existed for federal courts to assert pendent-party jurisdiction, 28 U.S.C. § 1367, Supplemental Jurisdiction. The present case remains the law for cases filed before December 1. This decision evidently prompted congressional dissatisfaction, leading Congress to make its intent clear.

NOTES:

NOTES

CHAPTER 10
REMOVAL JURISDICTION AND PROCEDURE

QUICK REFERENCE RULES OF LAW

1. **Removal Jurisdiction.** Congress has the power to enact statutes directing that certain state criminal prosecutions be removed to federal court. (Tennessee v. Davis)

NOTES

TENNESSEE v. DAVIS
100 U.S. 257 (1880).

NATURE OF CASE: Criminal prosecution for murder.

FACT SUMMARY: Davis (D), a federal revenue agent, was indicted for murder and scheduled for trial before a Tennessee (P) court. A federal law allowed prosecutions of revenue agents to be removed to federal court.

CONCISE RULE OF LAW: Congress has the power to enact statutes directing that certain state criminal prosecutions be removed to federal court.

FACTS: Davis (D), a federal revenue agent, was charged with murder in Tennessee (P). Prior to his trial before a state court, Davis (D) petitioned for removal to federal court, citing a federal law authorizing removal of any civil suit or criminal prosecution commenced against a revenue agent for conduct which occurred while acting under color of his office. Davis (P) claimed that the incident resulting in his indictment had occurred when he defended himself against shots fired at him while he was fulfilling his duty to confiscate an illegal distillery. Tennessee (P) opposed the petition for removal, claiming that the Constitution did not authorize Congress to enact the removal statute.

ISSUE: Does Congress have the constitutional authority to pass a law allowing certain state suits to be removed to federal court?

HOLDING AND DECISION: (Strong, J.) Yes. Congress has the power to enact statutes directing that certain state criminal prosecutions be removed to federal court. The Necessary and Proper Clause of the Constitution empowers Congress to pass laws facilitating the exercise of federal authority, including the judicial power. This latter power extends to all cases arising under the Constitution, the laws of the United States, and federal treaties. The right of Congress to authorize removal of state civil cases to federal court has long been recognized, and there is no reason why it should not have the same right with respect to criminal prosecutions. Removal statutes cannot be criticized as invasions of the sovereignty of the states, because the formation of the United States and the ratification of the Constitution contemplated a sacrifice of state autonomy. The statute enacted by Congress is not in conflict with the Constitution. Therefore, Davis' (D) petition for removal should be granted.

EDITOR'S ANALYSIS: At one time, it was recognized that Congress could authorize the removal of a state court action, but not prior to judgment. As Tennessee v. Davis illustrates, the right to authorize removal at even the earliest stages of litigation has long been acknowledged. Since 1815, federal officials have had a right to insist upon removal of state court actions which promise to be influenced by local bias. Today's removal statutes have been accorded a liberal construction by the courts, and Congress has provided for removal in numerous specific contexts.

NOTES:

NOTES

CHAPTER 11
JURISDICTIONAL AMOUNT

QUICK REFERENCE RULES OF LAW

1. **Diversity Claim Dismissal.** It must appear to a legal certainty that a diversity claim is really for less than the $10,000 jurisdictional floor in order to justify dismissal. (Nelson v. Keefer)

2. **Aggregate Claims.** Members of a class action cannot aggregate their claims in order to meet the required jurisdictional amount in federal courts. (Snyder v. Harris)

3. **Rule 23(b)(3) Class Action.** Each plaintiff in a Rule 23(b)(3) class action must satisfy the jurisdictional amount, and any plaintiff who does not must be dismissed from the case. (Zahn v. International Paper Co.)

NOTES

NELSON v. KEEFER

451 F.2d 289 (3rd Cir. 1971).

NOTES:

NATURE OF CASE: Appeal from dismissal of a personal injury diversity action.

FACT SUMMARY: The Nelsons (P) argued that if they were allowed to proceed to trial, they would be able to prove damage in excess of $10,000.

CONCISE RULE OF LAW: It must appear to a legal certainty that a diversity claim is really for less than the $10,000 jurisdictional floor in order to justify dismissal.

FACTS: Three members of the Nelson family were injured in an automobile accident allegedly caused by Keefer's (D) negligence. The son (P) suffered a thoracic lumbar sprain and after three years had incurred $136.28 in damages. Mrs. Nelson (P) incurred $258 in damages as a result of having suffered a hematoma of the skull, neck lash, and contusions of the right shoulder and ribs. Mr. Nelson (P) claimed $1,331.19 in damages, although his medical expenses did not appear to be related to the car accident. He did not claim lost wages. The Nelsons (P) filed their claim in federal court on the ground of diversity. The action was dismissed pre-trial because it appeared to the court that the claims were actually for less than the jurisdictional amount of $10,000. The Nelsons (P) appealed.

ISSUE: In order to justify dismissal, must it appear to a legal certainty that a diversity claim is really for less than the $10,000 jurisdictional floor?

HOLDING AND DECISION: (Aldisert, J.) Yes. It must appear to a legal certainty that a diversity claim is really for less than the $10,000 jurisdictional floor in order to justify dismissal. Federal diversity jurisdiction is available to hear "substantial claims" and thus Congress has set a minimum jurisdictional amount of $10,000. Although the Nelsons' (P) claim contained unliquidated damages, the claim must in good faith reach the jurisdictional requirement. If the upper limit of all actual and unspecified damages, such as pain and suffering, does not reach $10,000, then the claim may be dismissed. The Nelsons' (P) claim can, with a legal certainty, be said to fall below the federal jurisdictional requirement. Affirmed.

EDITOR'S ANALYSIS: The initial jurisdictional amount under the 1789 Judiciary Act was $500. In 1988 the jurisdictional amount was raised to $50,000. Until 1980 the jurisdictional amount requirement applied to federal questions as well as to diversity cases.

SNYDER v. HARRIS
GAS SERVICE COMPANY v. COBURN

394 U.S. 332 (1969).

NATURE OF CASE: (Snyder v. Harris) Action in fraud to recover money from wrongful sale of stock. (Gas Service Company v. Coburn) Action to recover money wrongfully collected by the Gas Service Company (D).

FACT SUMMARY: (Snyder v. Harris) Snyder (P) was not allowed to aggregate her claim with others in the class to meet the required jurisdictional amount. (Gas Service v. Coburn) Coburn was allowed to aggregate his claims with others in his class to meet the required amount.

CONCISE RULE OF LAW: Members of a class action cannot aggregate their claims in order to meet the required jurisdictional amount in federal courts.

FACTS: (Snyder v. Harris) Snyder (P) was a shareholder in the Missouri Fidelity Union Trust Insurance Company and brought this action to recover profits wrongfully acquired by the board of directors. The directors were paid an amount far in excess of the market value for their stock in order that the buyers could gain complete control of the company. Under Missouri law, the excess profit should properly be distributed among all the shareholders of the company. Snyder (P) brought this case in the Federal Court, alleging diversity of citizenship as the basis for federal jurisdiction. Snyder (P) only claimed $8,740 in damages, but contended that her claim should be aggregated with the other members of her class. Harris (D) moved to dismiss on the grounds that the matter in controversy did not exceed $10,000. The District Court granted the motion and the Court of Appeals for the Eighth Circuit affirmed. The case was appealed to the Supreme Court. (Gas Service Company v. Coburn) Coburn (P) brought this action to recover money the Gas Service Company (D) had collected as a city franchise tax from Coburn (P) and others living outside city limits. Coburn (P) only alleged damages of $7.81, but since he had filed a class action on behalf of 18,000 other people who had been overcharged, Coburn (P) alleged that the aggregation of all the claims would exceed $10,000. The Gas Company (0) moved to dismiss the case because the jurisdictional amount had not been mot but the court overruled the motion and the Court of Appeals for the Tenth Circuit affirmed. The decision was appealed to the Supreme Court.

ISSUE: Can distinct claims presented by various claimants in a class action be added together to provide the $10,000 jurisdictional amount in controversy?

HOLDING AND DECISION: No. Aggregation of claims has only been permitted in cases in which a single plaintiff seeks to aggregate two or more of his own claims against a single defendant and in cases in which two or more plaintiffs unite to enforce a single title or right in which they have a common and undivided interest. Before the 1966 amendment to Rule 23, class actions were divided into three classes. The true class actions were those in which the rights of the different class members were common and undivided and in such cases aggregation was permitted. The other two classes were not allowed to aggregate their claims as their claims were separate and distinct. The 1966 amendment did away with the old categories and replaced them with a functional approach to class actions. The amendment established new guidelines in allowing and controlling class actions. The Gas Service Company (D) argued that the amendment also changed the jurisdictional amount doctrine as well. The 1966 amendment to Rule 23 did not change the jurisdictional amount doctrine. The doctrine has been established for well over 100 years that separate claims cannot be aggregated to meet the jurisdictional amount. Congress has set the jurisdictional amount since 1789, and has raised the amount from time to time, the last time being in 1958, when the amount was raised to $10,000. Rule 82 of the FRCP states that these rules shall not be construed to extend or limit the jurisdiction of the United States District Courts. It is probable that Congress set the new amount with the fact in mind that separate claims could not be aggregated, although they didn't explicitly say so. It is argued that if separate claims are not allowed to be aggregated that many important federal question cases will not be heard in the Federal Courts. Also, that not allowing aggregation of claims will destroy the functional approach to class actions established by the 1966 amendment These arguments are not enough to overrule a precedent that has been established for such a long time. Most State Courts allow aggregation of claims and so many class actions such as these two cases can be brought in the State Courts. Finally, if there is a present need to expand the jurisdiction of the courts, the Constitution specifically vests that power in the Congress, not in the courts.

DISSENT: The dissent felt that the jurisdictional amount was mostly determined by rules set up by the courts and that there was no reason that the jurisdictional amount rules as to aggregation could not be reevaluated and possibly changed. They felt the majorities approach did destroy the effectiveness of the new class action rules. Claims should be allowed to be aggregated in order to allow people to bring class actions in the Federal Courts.

EDITOR'S ANALYSIS: There has been much criticism of the court's ruling in this case. Many feel, as do the dissenters, that the ruling destroys much of the effectiveness of the class action rules. The Supreme Court has upheld the ruling of this case in a more recent decision and they used the same rationale as they applied in this case. Because of these rulings, antitrust, securities, fraud and civil rights cases are the only types of class action cases heard in the Federal Courts now because they involve federal questions and no jurisdictional amount must be met.

NOTES:

ZAHN v. INTERNATIONAL PAPER CO.

414 U.S. 291 (1973).

NATURE OF CASE: Appeal from an order denying class action status based on lack of jurisdiction.

FACT SUMMARY: Zahn's (P) petition for class action certification was denied by the district court because not all members of the class claimed individual damages in excess of $10,000.

CONCISE RULE OF LAW: Each plaintiff in a Rule 23(b)(3) class action must satisfy the jurisdictional amount, and any plaintiff who does not must be dismissed from the case.

FACTS: Zahn (P), owner of property fronting on Lake Champlain, brought an action in district court on behalf of a class consisting of 200 lake-front property owners. They sought damages from International Paper Company (D) for allegedly having permitted discharges from its paper-making plant to flow into the lake. Plead as a diversity action based on 28 U.S.C.A. 1332, the court found that only the named plaintiffs satisfied the $10,000 jurisdictional amount, and refused to permit class action certification for failure to satisfy the jurisdictional amount. The court of appeals affirmed and Zahn (P) appealed.

ISSUE: Must each plaintiff in a Rule 23(b)(3) class action satisfy the jurisdictional amount?

HOLDING AND DECISION: (White, J.) Yes. Each plaintiff in a Rule 23(b)(3) class action must satisfy the jurisdictional amount, and any plaintiff who does not must be dismissed from the case. This rule plainly mandates not only that there may be no aggregation and that the entire case must be dismissed where none of the plaintiffs claims more than $10,000, but also requires that any plaintiff without the jurisdictional amount must be dismissed from the case, even though others allege jurisdictionally sufficient claims. We conclude that the court of appeals in this case accurately applied this well established rule. "One plaintiff may not ride on another's coattails." Affirmed.

DISSENT: (Brennan, Douglas, and Marshall, JJ.) The question in this case is not whether the class action must be permitted, but whether the district court has the power to determine whether to permit it, taking into account the elaborate guidance and discretion provided by Rule 23.

EDITOR'S ANALYSIS: It is well settled that in a class action only the citizenship of the named representatives is to be considered, and that it is no objection to jurisdiction that other members of the class, not named as parties, are of such citizenship as would defeat diversity. Supreme Tribe of Ben Hur v. Cauble, 1921, 41 S.Ct. 338, 255 U.S. 356, 65 L.Ed. 673. However, amount in controversy is clearly a different matter. The decisions of the present case and that of Snyder v. Harris, 89 S.Ct. 1053, 394 U.S. 332, 22 L.Ed.2d 319 (1969) have, in effect, made class actions unavailable in those cases in which more than $10,000 must be in controversy, notably diversity cases. For more on these two important cases, see 83 Harv. L. Rev. 202 (1969), 37 Tenn. L. Rev. 103 (1969), 22 U. Fla. L. Rev. 154, (1969), 24 U. Miami L. Rev. 173 (1969), 24 Sw. L. J. 354 (1970), 79 Yale L. J. 1577 (1970).

NOTES:

NOTES

CHAPTER 12
STATE SOVEREIGN IMMUNITY

QUICK REFERENCE RULES OF LAW

1. **Commerce Clause Power to Sue the States.** A state can be sued in federal court for monetary damages if the legislation creating the cause of action was passed pursuant to Congress□power under the Commerce Clause. (Pennsylvania v. Union Gas Co.)

2. **State Immunity.** A state official acting in violation of the Constitution is stripped of his state immunity and can be enjoined by a federal court. (Ex parte Young)

3. **Eleventh Amendment.** A suit by private parties seeking to impose liability, which must be paid from public funds in the state treasury, is barred by the Eleventh Amendment. (Edelman v. Jordan)

4. **Injunctions.** Federal courts may not issue an injunction against a state official based on state law. (Pennhurst State School & Hospital v. Halderman)

NOTES

PENNSYLVANIA v. UNION GAS COMPANY

491 U.S. 1 (1989).

NATURE OF CASE: Appeal from judgment permitting third-party complaint in CERCLA action.

FACT SUMMARY: After Union Gas Company (P) was sued by the United States for the cost of cleaning up environmental damage that was partially the State of Pennsylvania's (D) doing, it sought to hold the State (D) partially responsible.

CONCISE RULE OF LAW: A state can be sued in federal court for monetary damages if the legislation creating the cause of action was passed pursuant to Congress' power under the Commerce Clause.

FACTS: Union Gas (P) was involved with coal gasification that produced coal tar as a by-product. Union Gas (D) deposited the coal tar along Broadhead Creek. After Union Gas's (P) plant closed, the State of Pennsylvania (D) engaged in flood control activities along the creek. The State (D) struck the coal tar deposits while excavating the creek and caused the tar to contaminate the creek. The State (D) and the federal government cleaned up the tar. The federal government sued Union Gas (P) under CERCLA to recover the clean-up costs. Union Gas's (P) third-party complaint against the State (D) was dismissed by both the district court and the court of appeals. The Supreme Court remanded to re-examine in light of new legislation amending CERCLA, and the court of appeals found for Union Gas (P). The State (D) appealed, claiming Eleventh Amendment immunity. The Supreme Court granted certiorari.

ISSUE: Can a state be sued in federal court for monetary damages if the legislation creating the cause of action was passed pursuant to Congress' power under the Commerce Clause?

HOLDING AND DECISION: (Brennan, J.) Yes. A state can be sued in federal court for monetary damages is the legislation creating the cause of action was passed pursuant to Congress' power under the Commerce Clause. States have no sovereign immunity when they have surrendered it. By ratifying the Constitution, including the Commerce Clause, the states relinquished their authority to regulate commerce. To the extent they relinquished their authority, they also relinquished their immunity. There are occasions where monetary damages are the proper way for Congress to exert its power under the Commerce Clause. The Language of CERLA, as amended, clearly evinces an intent to hold liable for remedial efforts.

CONCURRENCE: (Stevens, J.) Although Congress does not have the power to abrogate the states' immunity, it does have plenary power to subject the states to suit in federal court.

CONCURRENCE: (White, J.) Congressional language in CERLA does not clearly abrogate the states' sovereign immunity. However, since the majority finds that it is clearly stated, I will concur.

CONCURRENCE AND DISSENT: (Scalia, J.) State sovereign immunity applies equally to federal question suits as to diversity suits. The federal government cannot give a private citizen the right to sue a state by legislation.

DISSENT: (O'Connor, J.) Congressional intent is nor clear enough to abrogate the states' sovereign immunity nor can Congress give a private citizen the right to sue a state by legislation.

EDITOR'S ANALYSIS: The diversity theory of the Eleventh Amendment contends that the Amendment was only meant as a bar against suits brought in federal courts against a state based on diversity jurisdiction. This theory would not grant a state sovereign immunity when a federal court action is based on either a federal question or admiralty law. The diversity theory arises out of attempts to explain why the language of the Amendment only addresses citizens of another state and not those of the state itself.

NOTES:

EX PARTE YOUNG

209 U.S. 123 (1908).

NATURE OF CASE: Habeas corpus proceeding following contempt order.

FACT SUMMARY: The Attorney General (D) of Minnesota was held in contempt for failing to comply with a federal court order to sue railroads for refusing to lower their rates.

CONCISE RULE OF LAW: A state official acting in violation of the Constitution is stripped of his state immunity and can be enjoined by a federal court.

FACTS: Minnesota passed a state statute reducing railroad rates. A federal court found the state statute in violation of the United States Constitution. The court then issued an injunction preventing state officers from enforcing the statute. When the Attorney General attempted to enforce it anyway, he was held in contempt of court. He then brought a habeas corpus proceeding claiming that the injunction was issued in violation of the Eleventh Amendment of the United States Constitution.

ISSUE: Is a state official acting in violation of the Constitution stripped of his state immunity, allowing him to be enjoined by a federal court?

HOLDING AND DECISION: (Peckham, J.) Yes. A state official, acting in violation of the Constitution, is stripped of his state immunity and can be enjoined by a federal court. The Eleventh Amendment prohibits one state from bringing an action against another. The Eleventh Amendment only applies when the state is the party of record. State officials carrying out state statutes are therefore immune from court action as well. However, when the state law they are carrying out has been held to be in violation of the United States Constitution, they are stripped of that immunity. The states cannot authorize their employees to violate the United States Constitution. Affirmed.

DISSENT: (Harlan, J.) The state cannot be present in a proceeding other than through its representatives. In this case, the federal injunction was necessarily against the state of Minnesota and thus in violation of the Eleventh Amendment.

EDITOR'S ANALYSIS: The Court's holding is based on its concern for companies having to defend themselves against actions that have already been declared unconstitutional. However, since the Constitution specifically prohibits states suing states, the court is evaluating the relative importance of the constitutional claims. The Eleventh Amendment comes out the loser.

NOTES:

EDELMAN v. JORDAN

415 U.S. 651 (1974).

NATURE OF CASE Appeal from an injunction requiring compliance with federal guidelines for paying AABD applicants.

FACT SUMMARY: Jordan (P) sued in federal court to enjoin Edelman (D) and the Illinois Dept. of Public Aid (IDPA) from noncompliance with federal guidelines for paying AABD social welfare payments. From a permanent injunction, Edelman (D) appealed.

CONCISE RULE OF LAW: A suit by private parties seeking to impose liability, which must be paid from public funds in the state treasury, is barred by the Eleventh Amendment.

FACTS: Jordan (P) sued in U.S. District Court to enjoin the Illinois Department of Public Aid (IDPA) and its director, Edelman (D), from noncompliance with federal guidelines for paying Aid to the Aged, Blind or Disabled (AABD) social welfare payments. The permanent injunction issued by the district court was affirmed by the Court of Appeals, and the Supreme Court granted certiorari.

ISSUE: Is a suit by a private party seeking to impose liability, which must be paid from public funds in the state treasury, barred by the Eleventh Amendment?

HOLDING AND DECISION: (Rehnquist, J.) Yes. A suit by private parties seeking to impose liability, which must be paid from public funds in the state treasury, is barred by the Eleventh Amendment. The Amendment provides: "The judicial power of the U.S. shall not be construed to extend to any suit in law or equity, commenced or prosecuted against one of the United States by Citizens of another state, or by Citizens or Subjects of any Foreign State." Even the landmark decision of Ex Parte Young does not extend so far as to permit a suit which seeks the award of an accrued monetary liability which must be met from the general revenues of the state, absent consent or waiver by the State of its Eleventh Amendment immunity, Therefore, the award of retroactive benefits by the District Court was improper. Reversed and remanded.

DISSENT: (Brennan, J.) Sovereign immunity in areas under which Congress has been granted specifically enumerated powers was surrendered when the Federal Union was formed.

DISSENT: (Douglas, J.) Once a state joins in a joint federal assistance program such as the one herein, it has waived its Eleventh Amendment rights and has consented to suit in federal court..

DISSENT: (Marshall, J.) The AABO is an attempt to induce state action in this area. It prescribes no standards/terms. However, the very voluntary nature of a state's participation in the program demonstrates a waiver of Eleventh Amendment rights. By agreeing to comply with the requirements of the Social Security Act and HEW regulations, the state has also agreed to subject itself to suit in federal courts to enforce such obligations. Congress intended relief for violations beyond merely cutting off aid. There is no showing that Congress intended to restrict any normal judicial remedies. Retroactive remedies must have been contemplated for otherwise state officials have nothing to lose by violating the Act.

EDITOR'S ANALYSIS: The right of the Federal Judiciary to summon a state as defendant and to adjudicate its rights and liabilities had been the subject of deep apprehension and of active debate at the time of the adoption of the Constitution, but the existence of any such right had been disclaimed by many of the most eminent advocates of the new federal government; it was largely owing to their successful dissipation of the fear of the existence of such federal power that the Constitution was finally adopted.

NOTES:

PENNHURST STATE SCHOOL AND HOSPITAL v. HALDERMAN

465 U.S. 89 (1984).

NATURE OF CASE: Appeal from damages and injunctive relief awarded in class action for violations of both the Fourteenth and Eighth Amendments.

FACT SUMMARY: Residents of Pennhurst Hospital (P) claimed that the care they were given violated their right to adequate habitation.

CONCISE RULE OF LAW: Federal courts may not issue an injunction against a state official based on state law.

FACTS: Halderman (P) and other residents (P) of Pennhurst State School and Hospital (D) brought suit against Pennhurst (D) and various state officials, claiming that the conditions of the school were so bad as to violate their rights under both the federal Constitution and state law. The district court found for the residents (P) and ordered that Pennhurst (D) be closed and the residents (P) resettled in the community. The court of appeals affirmed most of the order, but remanded for more detailed placement procedures. The Supreme Court reversed and remanded to the court of appeals to determine if the remedial order could be supported by state or federal law. On remand, the court of appeals found that the Pennsylvania Mental Health Act required the "least restricted environment" for the mentally retarded. Therefore it concluded that state law supported its prior order. Pennhurst (D) appealed to the U.S. Supreme Court, claiming that the Eleventh Amendment barred a federal court from granting an injunction against state officials on the basis of a pendent state-law claim.

ISSUE: May federal courts issue an injunction against a state official based on state law?

HOLDING AND DECISION: (Powell, J.) No. Federal courts may not issue an injunction against a state official based on state law. In this case, Pennhurst State officials (D) violated state law in carrying out their duties. Since there was no violation of federal law, the supremacy of the Constitution is not at issue. Absent an additional constitutional claim, the Eleventh Amendment prohibits federal courts from enforcing state law on state officials. Pendant claim jurisdiction is a judge-made doctrine and thus must be subject to the dictates of the Eleventh Amendment. The federal courts involved here lacked jurisdiction to issue the injunctions. Reversed.

DISSENT: (Brennan, J.) The bar of the Eleventh Amendment applies only to nonconstitutional claims against the states.

DISSENT: (Stevens, J.) The conduct of a state officer acting in contravention of state law is ultra vires and thus strips him of any sovereign immunity.

EDITOR'S ANALYSIS: The majority argues that the theory of Justices Stevens' dissent is a fiction that would always defeat state sovereign immunity. Justice Brennan's formulation of the Eleventh Amendment would alleviate the Court's concern for state courts enforcing federal dictates upon themselves. While each Justice is approaching the problem in a different way the principle is the same; sovereign immunity must take a back seat to federal interests.

NOTES:

CHAPTER 13
REMEDIES AGAINST STATE AND LOCAL ACTION: 42 U.S.C. § 1983

QUICK REFERENCE RULES OF LAW

1. **Civil Rights Act.** Congress intended § 1983 of the Civil Rights Act to give citizens a federal remedy for violations of rights granted by federal as well as state law. (Monroe v. Pape)

2. **Due Process Requirements.** State tort law remedies are sufficient to satisfy the due process requirements of the Fourteenth Amendment. (Parratt v. Taylor)

3. **Absolute Prosecutorial Immunity.** Absolute prosecutorial immunity applies only to activities that constitute a prosecutor's role in a judicial proceeding. (Burns v. Reed)

NOTES

MONROE v. PAPE

365 U.S. 167 (1961).

NATURE OF CASE: Appeal from dismissal of § 1983 complaint.

FACT SUMMARY: Chicago police officers (D) broke into Monroe's (P) home, searched it, arrested him, and held him for ten hours without a search warrant or a warrant for his arrest.

CONCISE RULE OF LAW: Congress intended § 1983 of the Civil Rights Act to give citizens a federal remedy for violations of rights granted by federal as well as state law.

FACTS: In the investigation of a murder, thirteen Chicago police officers (D) entered Monroe's (P) house and searched and ransacked every room in the house. Monroe (P) was taken to the police station without being charged. He was questioned for ten hours without being brought before a magistrate or being allowed to call an attorney. He was released without being charged. He subsequently brought suit against the police officers (D) and the City of Chicago (D). The district court dismissed the complaint for failure to state a cause of action. The court of appeals affirmed. The Supreme Court granted certiorari.

ISSUE: Did Congress intend § 1983 of the Civil Rights Act to give citizens a federal remedy for violations of rights granted by federal as well as state law?

HOLDING AND DECISION: (Douglas, J.) Yes. Congress intended § 1983 of the Civil Rights Act to give citizens a federal remedy for violations of rights granted by federal as well as state law. The purpose of § 1983 was to enforce the provision of the Fourteenth Amendment prohibiting violations occurring under color of authority. The City (D) claimed that the actions were not conducted under the color of authority since the Constitution of the State of Illinois prohibited the activity that the officers engaged in. Further, state law provided a remedy that Mr. Monroe (P) did not use. The purpose of § 1983 was to override state law in some circumstances and to provide an additional remedy when state law was inadequate and/or unavailable. Thus, the federal law is supplementary to the state remedy and can be availed of independent of the state remedy. Reversed.

CONCURRENCE: (Harlan, J.) The meaning of "under the color of any statute" should be upheld based on prior caselaw.

DISSENT: (Frankfurter, J.) Police officers violating state law cannot be held to be acting under color of state law.

EDITOR'S ANALYSIS: Justice Douglas's opinion comes out as it does largely because of the background against which the legislation was passed. The Civil Rights Act was also known as the Ku Klux Act in recognition of the framers' concern that states were unable to cope with the activities of the Klan in 1871. State remedies were adequate in theory but unavailable in practice because of the Klan's domination of state officials and judges in the south.

NOTES:

PARRATT v. TAYLOR

451 U.S. 527 (1981).

NATURE OF CASE: Appeal from grant of summary judgment in § 1983 action.

FACT SUMMARY: After Taylor (P), an inmate in a state correctional facility, ordered hobby materials which were lost, he claimed he had been deprived of his property without due process in violation of the Fourteenth Amendment.

CONCISE RULE OF LAW: State tort law remedies are sufficient to satisfy the due process requirements of the Fourteenth Amendment.

FACTS: Taylor (P) was a prisoner in a Nebraska state correctional facility. He ordered hobby materials through the mail and paid for them from his inmate account. When the packages arrived, two employees of the prison hobby center signed for them, contrary to established procedure. When Taylor (P) inquired after his materials, they could not be found. Taylor (P) brought suit in federal court under 42 U.S.C. § 1983 rather than under state tort law, contending that a violation of the Due Process Clause of the Fourteenth Amendment occurred due to negligence of the prison officials. The district court entered summary judgment in Taylor's (P) favor, and the court of appeals affirmed. The Supreme Court granted certiorari.

ISSUE: Are state tort law remedies sufficient to satisfy the due process requirements of the Fourteenth Amendment?

HOLDING AND DECISION: (Rehnquist, J.) Yes. State tort law remedies are sufficient to satisfy the due process requirements of the Fourteenth Amendment. The Fourteenth Amendment does not prevent all deprivations, only deprivations of property without due process of law. Post-deprivation remedies made available by a state may preclude a finding of a violation of the Fourteenth Amendment. In this case, the state provided a tort procedure whereby Taylor (P) could recoup the cost of the lost materials. The fact that the state remedy is not as expansive as the federal remedy does not mean that the state remedy does not satisfy the Due Process Clause. The state remedy (P) was available and adequate, and thus Taylor has not been deprived of due process of law. Reversed.

CONCURRENCE: (Powell, J.) Deprivation of property under the Due Process Clause requires an intentional act to deny something to someone.

CONCURRENCE AND DISSENT: (Marshall, J.) Because Taylor (P) is a prisoner, the Court should not assume that he was informed of the adequate state remedy available to him.

EDITOR'S ANALYSIS: In Daniels v. Williams, 474 U.S. 327 (1986), the Court partially overruled Parratt, stating that a negligent act can not implicate the Due Process Clause. In that case a prisoner claimed that his due process rights were violated when he was injured by a prison guard's negligence. The Daniels Court understood the word "deprive" to require an actual abuse of power.

NOTES:

BURNS v. REED

500 U.S. 478 (1991).

NATURE OF CASE: Appeal from directed verdict for defendant in § 1983 action for compensatory and punitive damages.

NOTES:

FACT SUMMARY: After Reed (D), a prosecutor, gave the police advice on their murder investigation of Burns (P) and participated in her probable cause hearing, he claimed absolute immunity when sued by Burns (P).

CONCISE RULE OF LAW: Absolute prosecutorial immunity applies only to activities that constitute a prosecutor's role in a judicial proceeding.

FACTS: Burns (P) called the police in connection with the shooting of her two sons. The police suspected her of committing the murders despite her continual denials and exculpatory evidence. The investigating officers asked Chief Deputy Prosecutor Reed's (D) advice on whether to hypnotize Burns (P). Reed (D) assured the officers that they could hypnotize her. Under hypnosis, Burns (P) referred to herself and the assailant using the same name. At the probable cause hearing, the judge issued a warrant based upon the testimony that Burns (P) had confessed to the murders. Neither Reed (D) nor the police informed the judge that this confession was obtained while she was hypnotized. The trial court subsequently suppressed the statements made under hypnosis and Reed (D) dropped all charges. Burns (P) then brought suit against Reed (D) for violations of her constitutional rights. Both the trial court and the court of appeals found that Reed (D) had absolute prosecutorial immunity. Burns (P) appealed.

ISSUE: Does absolute prosecutorial immunity apply only to activities that constitute a prosecutor's role in judicial proceeding?

HOLDING AND DECISION: (White, J.) Yes. Absolute prosecutorial immunity applies only to activities that constitute a prosecutor's role in a judicial proceeding. Issuing of a search warrant is a judicial act. Potential liability for participating in such an act would interfere with the goal of prosecutorial independence. Thus Reed (D) is absolutely immune from any liability related to his participation in the probable cause hearing. However, the advice that Reed (D) gave to the officers was not intimately related to the judicial process since it involved the investigative stage of the case. Thus, with respect to this behavior, Reed (D) is entitled to qualified immunity. Affirmed in part and reversed in part.

CONCURRENCE AND DISSENT: (Scalia, J.) Reed's initiation of the probable cause hearing also involved a constitutional violation would have only received qualified immunity, and thus should have been considered by the Court.

EDITOR'S ANALYSIS: Part of the rationale for not extending total immunity to the advice given to police officers is that qualified immunity will force prosecutors to do exactly what we want them to do; i.e., think twice before giving out legal advice. A police officer, it should be noted, would only be granted qualified immunity for following the advice of the prosecutor.

NOTES

CHAPTER 14
ABSTENTION

QUICK REFERENCE RULES OF LAW

1. **Federal Court Abstention.** Federal courts should abstain from deciding cases involving issues of state law which can easily be resolved by a state court. (Railroad Commission of Texas v. Pullman Co.)

2. **Uncertain Question of State Law.** Federal courts must not abstain from exercising jurisdiction unless there is an uncertain question of state law. (Hawaii Housing Authority v. Midkiff)

3. **Eminent Domain Proceedings.** A district court sitting in diversity may stay an eminent domain proceeding pending state court interpretation of the power to condemn. (Louisiana Power & Light Co. v. City of Thibodaux)

4. **Refusal.** Even though a federal court has jurisdiction of a particular proceeding, it may, in its sound discretion, refuse to enforce or protect legal rights, the exercise of which may be prejudiced to the public interest. (Burford v. Sun Oil Co.)

5. **Concurrent State Proceedings.** The existence of concurrent state court proceedings does not require a federal court to abstain from exercising jurisdiction absent exceptional circumstances. (Colorado River Water Conservation District v. United States)

6. **The Abstention Doctrine.** Where, but for the abstention doctrine, the primary factual determination would be made in the district court, the state court ruling may be subjected to a de novo review by the district court unless all claims have been unreservedly submitted to the state court and were fully litigated there. (England v. Louisiana State Board of Medical Examiners)

NOTES

RAILROAD COMM'N OF TEXAS v. PULLMAN CO.

312 U.S. 496 (1941).

NATURE OF CASE: Suit seeking injunctive relief.

FACT SUMMARY: An order of the Railroad Commission (D) required that a conductor, rather than a porter, be in charge of all Pullman (P) cars.

CONCISE RULE OF LAW: Federal courts should abstain from deciding cases involving issues of state law which can easily be resolved by a state court.

FACTS: When passenger traffic was light, certain trains operating in Texas were served by only one sleeping car. On these occasions, the cars were supervised by the porters (P), most of whom were black, instead of by conductors, who were white. In response to this situation, the Railroad Commission of Texas (D) promulgated an order which forbade the operation of sleeping cars unless they were continuously in the charge of a conductor. The Pullman Company (P), which manufactured sleeping cars, together with the railroads (P) affected, brought suit in federal district court to enjoin the Commission's (D) order, and the porters (P) were permitted to intervene in the action. The railroads (P) and the Pullman Company (P) contended that the order contravened Texas law as well as the federal Constitution. The porters (P) argued that the discriminatory effects of the order violated the Fourteenth Amendment. A three-judge panel enjoined enforcement of the order, denying that the applicable Texas statutes sustained the Commission's (D) injunction.

ISSUE: Should federal courts resolve issues of state law which could be decided by state courts?

HOLDING AND DECISION: (Frankfurter, J.) No. Federal courts should abstain from deciding cases involving issues of state law which can easily be resolved by a state court. The porters (P) have raised a significant constitutional issue, but they have also touched upon a sensitive social question of considerable moment. It is preferable that the case be resolved by resort to state law, rather than by determining the merits of the constitutional issue. The outcome can turn on whether or not the contested order is consistent with the Commission's (D) authority to prevent discrimination and other abuses. A state court may determine whether or not the order is within the ambit of the Commission's (D) authority, thus precluding the necessity for a federal court to decide the case in a manner which might ultimately create friction between state and federal law. Since Texas law facilitates a state court resolution of this dispute, the federal action should not be given effect until the appropriate Texas court has had a chance to consider the merits of this controversy.

EDITOR'S ANALYSIS: The abstention doctrine compels federal courts to refrain, at least temporarily, from deciding cases which may be resolved by reference to state law or which require a preliminary consideration of state law issues. The doctrine had been recognized and applied in cases which predated the Pullman Company case, and has been utilized by subsequent cases as well. The purpose of the doctrine is to insure that federal courts will not interfere with their state counterparts by rendering decisions which are inconsistent with ultimate state court resolutions of identical issues.

NOTES:

HAWAII HOUSING AUTHORITY v. MIDKIFF

467 U.S. 229 (1984).

NATURE OF CASE: Appeal from district court exercise of jurisdiction in constitutional challenge to state land reform statute.

FACT SUMMARY: The Hawaiian Housing Authority (P) condemned lands and transferred them to the existing lessees, resulting in a suit filed by Midkiff (P) and other owners (P) to declare the state law authorizing the transfers unconstitutional.

CONCISE RULE OF LAW: Federal courts must not abstain from exercising jurisdiction unless there is an uncertain question of state law.

FACTS: The Hawaii legislature passed an act that allowed the Housing Authority (D) to condemn lands and then transfer them to current lessees. The Land Reform Act was passed in an attempt to break up concentrated property ownership. Rather than comply with the condemnation proceedings, Midkiff (P) and other landholders (P) brought suit, claiming the Act was unconstitutional. The district court accepted jurisdiction and found the Act constitutional. The court of appeals agreed that jurisdiction was proper but reversed the district court's holding. The Supreme Court granted certiorari.

ISSUE: Must federal courts generally not abstain from exercising jurisdiction?

HOLDING AND DECISION: (O'Connor, J.) No. Federal courts must not abstain from exercising jurisdiction unless there is an uncertain question of state law. Federalism requires that federal courts abstain from deciding unsettled questions of state law. This policy is based on a desire to avoid federal litigation whenever possible and to prevent friction between the states and the federal system. Here, the Land Reform Act does not raise any questions of state law. Federal courts should not abstain from jurisdiction because there is a possible state issue — the state issue should be obvious. Decision not to abstain affirmed.

EDITOR'S ANALYSIS: in Brockett v. Spokane Arcades, Inc., 472 U.S. 491 (1985), the Court used the same underlying principals to find that a court should abstain from accepting jurisdiction when the language of a state law could be interpreted in a way to foreclose further federal litigation.

NOTES:

LOUISIANA POWER & LIGHT CO. v. CITY OF THIOBODAUX

360 U.S. 25 (1959).

NATURE OF CASE: Appeal from order staying eminent domain proceedings.

FACT SUMMARY: When the City of Thibodaux (D) filed a petition of eminent domain against Louisiana Power and Light (D), a Florida corporation, it removed the proceeding to federal court on the basis of diversity.

CONCISE RULE OF LAW: A district court sitting in diversity may stay an eminent domain proceeding pending state court interpretation of the power to condemn.

FACTS: The City of Thibodaux (P) filed a petition of expropriation against Lousiana Power and Light (D), a Florida corporation. Power and Light (D) removed to a federal court based on diversity jurisdiction. The district court stayed the proceeding so that the Supreme Court of Louisiana could interpret state law authorizing the City's (P) power to exercise eminent domain. The court of appeals reversed on the grounds that there were no circumstances justifying use of the staying procedure. The Supreme Court granted certiorari.

ISSUE: May a district court, sitting in diversity, stay an eminent domain proceeding pending state court interpretation of the taking authority?

HOLDING AND DECISION: (Frankfurter, J.) Yes. A district court, sitting in diversity, may stay an eminent domain proceeding pending state court interpretation of the power to condemn. Expropriations by their nature are issues of state law. On the other hand, a federal court should not give up jurisdiction merely because a difficult question of state law is involved. However, the eminent domain issue turns on legislation with much local variation interpreted in local settings. The state courts are best able to interpret this issue. Thus, staying the proceedings is the proper course of action for the district court. The court has not given up its jurisdiction or been remiss in its judicial duties; it will ultimately award compensation if the taking is sustained. The court of appeals' decision is reversed, and the stay order is reinstated.

CONCURRENCE: (Stewart, J.) The stay of proceeding is clearly within the district court's discretion.

DISSENT: (Brennan, J.) The procedure used by the district court is only to be used in two exceptional circumstances: to avoid deciding unnecessary constitutional issues or to prevent friction between the federal system and the states. Neither is applicable here.

EDITOR'S ANALYSIS: The same day it decided the above case, the Court also handed down a decision in County of Allegheny v. Mashuda Co., 360 U.S. 185 (1959). In Mashuda, the County had condemned certain property that it then leased to a private business, which was against state law. The Mashuda Court concluded that since the controlling state law was clear, the district court could not refrain from prompt adjudication of the case, the eminent domain issue notwithstanding. In his dissent in Thibodaux, Justice Brennan maintained that the majority's assumption that the special nature of eminent domain always entailed federal-state friction was a specious argument and "totally at war' with the Court's holding in Mashuda.

NOTES:

BURFORD v. SUN OIL CO.

319 U.S. 315 (1943).

NATURE OF CASE: Appeal from an action seeking an injunction.

FACT SUMMARY: A federal district court dismissed an action brought by the Sun Oil Go. (P) against the Railroad Commission of Texas, seeking to enjoin the execution of the Commission's order permitting the drilling and operation of certain oil wells and alleging denial of due process of law.

CONCISE RULE OF LAW: Even though a federal court has jurisdiction of a particular proceeding, it may, in its sound discretion, refuse to enforce or protect legal rights, the exercise of which may be prejudiced to the public interest.

FACTS: Sun Oil Co. (P) brought an action in a federal district court attacking the validity of an order of the Texas Railroad Commission. The Texas Railroad Commission had granted Burford (D) a permit to drill four wells on a small plot of land in the East Texas oil field. Sun Oil Co. (P) seeks to enjoin the execution of this order. Jurisdiction of the federal court was invoked because of the diversity of citizenship of the parties and because Sun Oil Co. (P) contended that the order denied them due process of law. The district court dismissed the complaint of Sun Oil Co. (P). The court of appeals reversed the judgment and granted Sun Oil's (P) injunction. Burford (D) appealed to the Supreme Court.

ISSUE: Assuming that the federal district court had jurisdiction, should it, as a matter of sound equitable discretion, have declined to exercise that jurisdiction?

HOLDING AND DECISION: (Black, J.) Yes. The Order under consideration is part of the general regulatory system devised for the conservation of oil and gas in Texas. The federal government has chosen to leave the principal regulatory responsibilities of these large oil fields with the states. The standards applied by the Commission in a given case necessarily affect the entire state conservation system. The over-all plan of regulation is of vital interest to the general public which must be assured that the speculative interests of individual owners will be put aside when necessary to prevent the irretrievable loss of oil in other parts of the field. With full knowledge of the importance of the decisions of the Railroads Commission both to the state and to oil operators, the Texas legislature has established a system of thorough judicial review by its own state courts. Texas courts can give fully as great relief, including temporary restraining orders, as the federal courts. Delay, misunderstanding of local law, and needless federal conflict with the state policy, are the inevitable product of a double system of review. Furthermore, if the plaintiff in the instant case follows the state procedure from the Commission to the state supreme court, ultimate review of the federal question of due process is fully preserved in this court. Past cases reflect a doctrine of abstention whereby federal courts, exercising a wise discretion, restrain their authority leaving problems of state law to state courts. This case, involving as it does basic problems of Texas' conservation and regulation of natural resources, is intricately bound up with state policy and requires the exercise of the district court's equitable discretion, so that Texas courts have the first opportunity to consider these important questions. Therefore, the decision of the court of appeals is reversed and the judgment of the district court dismissing the complaint is affirmed.

CONCURRENCE: (Douglas, J.) The Texas courts do not sit merely to enforce rights based on orders of the state administrative agency. They sit in judgment of that agency. If the federal courts undertook to sit in review of this state agency, they would in effect actively participate in the fashioning of the state's domestic policy.

DISSENT: (Frankfurter, J. joined by Roberts and Reed, JJ. and the Chief Justice) To deny a suitor access to a federal district court under the circumstances of this case is to disregard a duty enjoined by Congress based on diversity of citizenship between parties. Furthermore, it has never been questioned that a right created by state law and enforceable in state courts can also be enforced in the federal courts where the parties to the controversy are citizens of different states. The duty of the judiciary is to exercise the jurisdiction which Congress has conferred, to do otherwise is to assume a legislative role best left to Congress.

EDITOR'S ANALYSIS: Historically speaking, there has existed an unspoken rule, enunciated by Chief Justice Marshall in 1 824, that the federal judiciary will not assume jurisdiction if it should not but that if it should it must take jurisdiction. It is quite evident that no such rule is employed by the federal courts today. The development of the abstention doctrine has led to a recognition of situations under which a federal court may decline jurisdiction even though granted by the Constitution and Congressional statutes. One type of situation was evidenced in Burford where the federal court abstained to avoid needless conflict with complex state administrative regulations. In these circumstances the usual course followed is for the court to dismiss the case rather than retain jurisdiction, pending a determination by the state courts.

NOTES:

COLORADO RIVER WATER CONSERVATION DISTRICT v. UNITED STATES

424 U.S. 800 (1976).

NATURE OF CASE: Appeal from dismissal of an action to determine federal water rights.

FACT SUMMARY: After the United States (P) filed a suit in federal court to assert its reserved water rights against state water users (D), the defendants filed suit in state court to adjudicate all the water claims, state and federal.

CONCISE RULE OF LAW: The existence of concurrent state court proceedings does not require a federal court to abstain from exercising jurisdiction absent exceptional circumstances.

FACTS: Under the McCarren Amendment, the federal government consented to be joined as a defendant under state law adjudication of water rights. The State of Colorado established seven water districts to manage the adjudication of water claims. The United States government (P) was involved in water adjudication in several districts. The government (P) instituted a claim for reserved Indian water rights in division 7 in the federal district court, which was located 300 miles from the division. Over 1,000 state water users (D) were included in the litigation. One of the users (D) moved to have the government's (P) federal claim joined to the state court proceeding and then served the federal government (P) under the McCarren Act. Its motion to dismiss the federal court action was also granted. The court of appeals, however, found the abstention inappropriate and reversed. The defendants appealed, and the Supreme Court granted certiorari.

ISSUE: Does the existence of concurrent state court proceedings require a federal court to abstain from exercising jurisdiction absent exceptional circumstances?

HOLDING AND DECISION: (Brennan, J.) No. The existence of concurrent state court proceedings do not require a federal court to abstain from exercising jurisdiction absent exceptional circumstances. However, under the McCarran Amendment, the federal government instituted a policy designed to avoid piecemeal water rights litigation. The distance to the federal court, the number of state claims involved, and the federal government's involvement with the state proceeding establish exceptional circumstances allowing the federal district court to abstain from exercising jurisdiction in this case. The federal suit was properly dismissed. Reversed.

DISSENT: (Stewart, J.) The district court had jurisdiction, and the circumstances of the case did not warrant dismissal of the case.

EDITOR'S ANALYSIS: The above decision has been criticized as mere "docket clearing," based solely on judicial convenience and employing criteria that impermissibly expand the traditional scope of the abstention doctrine. See Mullenix, 75 Geo. L.J. 99 (1966). By formulating additional circumstances to justify abstention, the Court has encroached on the rights of federal litigants, Mullenix argues, without a compelling justification grounded in federal-state friction.

NOTES:

ENGLAND v. LOUISIANA STATE BOARD OF MEDICAL EXAMINERS

375 U.S. 411 (1964).

NATURE OF CASE: Constitutional challenge to state law.

NOTES:

FACT SUMMARY: The District Court referred a constitutional challenge to a state medical licensing statute to state court based on the doctrine of abstention.

CONCISE RULE OF LAW: Where, but for the abstention doctrine, the primary factual determination would be made in the district court, the state court ruling may be subjected to a de novo review by the district court unless all claims have been unreservedly submitted to the state court and were fully litigated there.

FACTS: England (P) and other chiropractors brought suit in district court challenging the constitutionality of Louisiana's (D) medical licensing statutes. The district court abstained requiring that the case be referred to the state court for a determination of whether its medical licensing statute applied to chiropractors. Instead, England (P) had all federal questions fully litigated by the state courts which upheld the statute finding that it applied to chiropractors. The case was then brought back to the district court which refused to hear it since all federal question issues had been decided. The district court alleged that the proper procedure was to appeal the decision to the U.S. Supreme Court.

ISSUE: May a District Court grant a de novo hearing, after abstention, if all federal issues were submitted and fully tried by the state court?

HOLDING AND DECISION: No. In cases where the need to litigate federal questions may be deviated by a finding by the state courts that a challenged statute does not apply to plaintiff, it is proper for the federal court to abstain pending such a determination. The action is submitted to state court, which is informed of the basis of plaintiff's claim and that the matter is pending in federal court. The state court merely determines, based on plaintiff's claim, whether the statute applies. It does not reach the federal question. The case is then returned to district court for a de novo trial since a plaintiff choosing federal court cannot be forced to litigate the issues in state court, thereby being denied the benefit of federal factfinding. However, if plaintiff voluntarily submits all questions to the state court that fully litigates them, plaintiff has waived district court review, and the case must be appealed here. This case is remanded to the district court only because of the confusion in the law that caused England's (P) mistake. Reversed.

EDITOR'S ANALYSIS: Abstention is generally applied for two basic reasons. If a statute does not apply, it is a needless expenditure of judicial resources to try the entire case. Secondly, abstention is consistent with two federal judicial policies; i.e., deciding cases on the narrowest basis so as not having to declare acts to be unconstitutional and deference to state law and determinations construing the reach of its statutes. The chief criticism of the doctrine is that it is both costly and time consuming. It took nine years to reach the merits in England.

CHAPTER 15
ANTI-INJUNCTION ACT

QUICK REFERENCE RULES OF LAW

1. **Claim in Controversy and Prior Adjudication.** A federal court does not have the power to stay a proceeding in a state court simply because the claim in controversy has previously been adjudicated in the federal court. (Toucey v. New York Life Insurance Co.)

2. **Res Judicata.** A federal court is empowered to stay proceedings in a state court when necessary to protect or effectuate its judgments if the state court has not yet ruled on the merits of the res judicata issue. (Parsons Steel, Inc. v. First Alabama Bank)

3. **42 U.S.C.A. 1983.** 42 U.S.C.A. 1983 is an "Act of Congress" which comes within the "expressly authorized" exception of the anti-injunction statute (28 U.S.C.A. 2283) so as to permit a federal court to grant an injunction to stay proceedings pending in a state court. (Mitchum v. Foster)

4. **In Rem Cases.** The state or federal court that first acquires jurisdiction in an in rem case has exclusive authority to decide the dispute. (Kline v. Burke Construction Co.)

NOTES

TOUCEY v. NEW YORK LIFE INSURANCE CO.

314 U.S. 118, 62 S.Ct. 139 (1941).

NATURE OF CASE: Appeal from injunction of state court proceedings in a a suit for fraud and unlawful cancelation of insurance policy.

FACT SUMMARY: Toucey (P) claimed that New York Life (D) fraudulently deprived him of disability payments, but the court ruled against him, prompting a federal court to dismiss a subsequent state action based on res judicata.

CONCISE RULE OF LAW: A federal court does not have the power to stay a proceeding in a state court simply because the claim in controversy has previously been adjudicated in the federal court.

FACTS: Toucey (P) claimed that when he became disabled, New York Life (D) canceled his policy unlawfully and fraudulently concealed the disability provision of his policy. When he discovered the disability provisions, he filed a claim and was rejected. Toucey (P) then brought suit in state court. New York Life (D) petitioned for removal to federal court. The federal court found no fraud and no disability and dimissed the case. Toucey (P) did not appeal. Two years later, an assignee of Toucey (P) filed suit in state court against New York Life (D) alleging that Toucey's (P) disability entitled him to payment of the benefits. New York Life (D) filed a supplemental bill in federal court requesting an injunction to be issued to prevent the state court from deciding the case before it. The original injunction was granted, and the court of appeals affirmed it. Toucey (P) appealed. The Supreme Court granted certiorari.

ISSUE: Does a federal court have the power to stay a proceeding in a state court simply because the claim in controversy has previously been adjudicated in federal court?

HOLDING AND DECISION: (O'Connor, J.) No. A federal court does not have the power to stay a proceeding in a state court simply because the claim in controversy has previously been adjudicated in the federal court. Section 265 of the Judicial Code prohibits federal courts from enjoining state court proceedings. The purpose of this section is to free state courts from the interference of the federal judiciary. Other than the statutory exception to this rule the only other exception is where the federal court has taken possession of the property in an in rem proceeding. The rationale for this exception is that if it were not in place, there would be unnecessary friction between the states and federal courts. However, just because there are exceptions to § 265 is no justification for making another. Reversed.

DISSENT: (Reed, J.) Injunctions are the means by which federal courts enforce their judgments and thus they are necessary to the principle of res judicata.

EDITOR'S ANALYSIS: Congress subsequently overruled Toucey by revising the language of the Anti-Injunction Act to allow a federal court to enjoin a state court proceeding "where necessary to protect or effectuate its judgments." The Reviser's Note appended to the 1948 revision stated that, prior to Toucey, the power of the federal courts to protect their judgments was unquestioned. By reinstating the so=called "relitigation exception," the revisers sought to protect what they regarded as superior federal interests.

NOTES:

PARSONS STEEL, INC. v. FIRST ALABAMA BANK

106 S.Ct. 768, 88 L.Ed.2d 877 (1986).

NATURE OF CASE: Review of a federal decision to enjoin prosecution of a state action.

FACT SUMMARY: First Alabama Bank (D) obtained a federal judgment enjoining prosecution of a state action by Parsons Steel (P) even though the state court ruled that res judicata did not bar the state action.

CONCISE RULE OF LAW: A federal court is empowered to stay proceedings in a state court when necessary to protect or effectuate its judgments if the state court has not yet ruled on the merits of the res judicata issue.

FACTS: Parsons Steel (P) first instituted an action against First Alabama Bank (D) in Alabama state court and then filed a suit in federal court a few months later alleging the same conduct that was the subject of the state-court suit also violated federal law. The final judgment in state court was in favor of First Alabama Bank (D), but the state court ruled that res judicata did not bar the state action. First Alabama Bank (D) went to federal court and obtained an injunction against further prosecution of the state proceedings based on the notion that the state judgment effectively nullified the earlier federal-court judgment in favor of First Alabama Bank (D). From a court of appeals decision upholding the injunction, Parsons Steel (P) sought review by certiorari.

ISSUE: Can a federal court stay state court proceedings when such is necessary to protect or effectuate its judgments?

HOLDING AND DECISION: (Rehnquist, J.) Yes. The federal Anti-Injunction Act precludes a federal court from staying state court proceedings except as expressly authorized by Congressional act or where necessary in aid of its jurisdiction or to protect or effectuate its judgments. It is clear that the limited exception set forth in the Anti-Injunction Act applies to those situations in which the state court has not yet ruled on the merits of the res judicata issue. If the state court has ruled that res judicata does not bar the state proceedings, the full faith and credit clause comes into play and the federal courts must turn to state law to determine the preclusive effect of the state court's decision. The district court is best situated to determine and apply Alabama preclusion law in the first instance. Reversed and remanded for further proceedings.

EDITOR'S ANALYSIS: There is still a procedural route available to challenge the state court's res judicata decision. First, the appellate route must be traversed in the state court system. Then, f rom the final state appellate decision, the proper mechanism is a petition for certiorari to the United States Supreme Court.

MITCHUM v. FOSTER

407 U.S. 225 (1972).

NATURE OF CASE: Direct appeal from an order of the court of appeals denying an injunction against state court proceedings.

FACT SUMMARY: Mitchum (D) sought an injunction against state proceedings he alleged had unconstitutionally ordered his bookstore closed. The court of appeals refused to enjoin, and Foster (D) appealed directly to the Supreme Court.

CONCISE RULE OF LAW: 42 U.S.C.A. 1983 is an "Act of Congress" which comes within the "expressly authorized" exception of the anti-injunction statute (28 U.S.C.A. 2283) so as to permit a federal court to grant an injunction to stay proceedings pending in a state court.

FACTS: The Florida prosecutor brought a proceeding in state court to close down Mitchum's (D) bookstore as a public nuisance under Florida law. The state court preliminarily enjoined operation of the bookstore, and Mitchum (D) brought an action in U.S. District Court alleging the state officials were depriving him of rights protected by the First and Fourteenth Amendments. Relying on 42 U.S.C.A. 1983 he sought an injunction against the state court proceedings. The district court ordered a temporary injunction, the court of appeals dissolved the injunction, and Mitchum (D) appealed directly to the Court.

ISSUE: Is 42 U.S.C.A. 1983 an "Act of Congress" which comes within the "expressly authorized" exception of the federal anti-injunction statute so as to permit a federal court to grant an injunction to stay proceedings pending in a state court?

HOLDING AND DECISION: (Stewart, J.) Yes. 42 U.S.C.A. 1983 is an "Act of Congress" which comes within the "expressly authorized" exception of the anti-injunction statute so as to permit a federal court to grant an injunction to stay proceedings pending in a state court. The test is whether an act of Congress, clearly creating a federal right or remedy enforceable in a federal court of equity, could be given its intended scope only by the stay of a state court proceeding. The very purpose of § 1983 was to interpose the federal courts between the states and the people as guardians of the people's federal rights — to protect the people from unconstitutional action under color of state law "whether that action be executive, legislative, or judicial." In carrying out that purpose, Congress plainly authorized the federal courts to issue injunctions in § 1983 actions by expressly authorizing a "suit in equity" as one of the means of redress. For these reasons we conclude that § 1983 is an act of Congress that falls within the "expressly authorized" exception of the anti-injunction statute. Reversed and remanded.

EDITOR'S ANALYSIS: This case is the third in the trilogy of the Court's interpretation of § 2283. The opinion here decidedly favors the "flexible" interpretation of § 2283. Compare Baines v. City of Danville, 337 F.2d 579 (4th Cir., 1964), where Judge Haynsworth noted that since § 2283 had been "fathered by the principles of comity," it "should be read in the light of those principles and, though absolute in its terms, is inapplicable in extraordinary cases in which an injunction against state court proceedings is the only means of avoiding grave and irreparable injury."

NOTES:

KLINE v. BURKE CONSTRUCTION CO.

260 U.S. 226 (1922).

NATURE OF CASE: Review of order enjoining prosecution of breach of contract suit in state court.

FACT SUMMARY: Burke Construction (P) sought to enjoin Kline (D) from suing the company in state court over a contract on which Burke (P) had based its federal diversity suit.

CONCISE RULE OF LAW: The state or federal court that first acquires jurisdiction in an in rem case has exclusive authority to decide the dispute.

FACTS: Burke (P) brought a breach of contract action against Kline (D) in federal district court based on diversity of citizenship. After this suit was underway, Kline (D) brought its own suit in equity in state court alleging that Burke (P) had abandoned the contract. The second case was based on the same facts and alleged the same cause of action, but it included additional parties. The federal suit was declared a mistrial. Burke (P) filed a dependent complaint asking the district court to enjoin the state court proceedings. The district court refused to grant the injunction. However, the court of appeals reversed and remanded to the district court with an order to issue the injunction. Kline (D) appealed.

ISSUE: Does the state or federal court that first acquires jurisdiction in an in rem case have exclusive authority to decide the dispute?

HOLDING AND DECISION: (Sutherland, J.) Yes. The state or federal court that first acquires jurisdiction in an in rem case has exclusive authority to decide the dispute. However, if an action is in personam, then a similar second action in a different jurisdiction is not precluded. A federal court is permitted to enjoin a similar state proceeding in an in rem action when the federal court has taken possession of the res first in order to avoid friction between the two court systems. But the same justification does not apply when the action, like the instant case, is in personam and only claims monetary damages. Burke (P) argues that this procedure potentially deprives it of its right to maintain an action in federal court under the Constitution. But the right to bring a suit in diversity is not a constitutional right. Therefore, any res judicata effect from the state court cannot deprive Burke (P) of its constitutional right to invoke the jurisdiction of the federal court. Reversed.

EDITOR'S ANALYSIS: In Atlantic Cost Line R.R. v. Brotherhood of Locomotive Engineers, 398 U.S. 281(1970), the Court interpreted the "in aid of jurisdiction" exception to the Anti-injunction Act as preventing the severe disruption of the federal court exercising jurisdiction. In that case, a federal court had granted an injunction against a state court injunction preventing union members from picketing. The Court, however, concluded that the state and federal courts had concurrent jurisdiction and neither court could prevent management or the union from pursuing claims in both courts. The "in aid of jurisdiction" exception, it ruled, may only be invoked when state court interference seriously impairs the federal court's flexibility and authority to decide a case.

NOTES:

CHAPTER 16
"OUR FEDERALISM"

QUICK REFERENCE RULES OF LAW

1. **Federal Court Interference.** Federal courts should not interfere with pending state court proceedings except where it can be shown that the defendant will suffer irreparable injury. (Younger v. Harris)

2. **Federal Court Interference.** Once a state criminal prosecution has commenced, a federal court should not issue a declaratory judgment in the case unless, under the circumstances, injunctive relief would be appropriate. (Samuels v. Mackell)

3. **Declaratory Judgment Act.** Under the Declaratory Judgment Act, declaratory relief is intended to act as an alternative to injunctions and to be utilized to test the constitutionality of state criminal statutes in cases where injunctive relief would be unavailable. (Steffel v. Thompson)

4. **Preclusion of Federal Declaratory or Injunctive Relief.** The rule that federal declaratory or injunctive relief is generally precluded if a state criminal charge is pending encompasses the situation where the state criminal charge is filed any time subsequent to commencement of the federal action but “before any proceedings of substance on the merits have taken place in the federal court.” (Hicks v. Miranda)

5. **Federal Court Interference.** In actions seeking injunctive relief from the execution of a state court judgment pending appeal in the state courts, federal courts should abstain if the grant of relief would constitute a significant intrusion on the state's judicial system. (Pennzoil Co. v. Texaco, Inc.)

NOTES

YOUNGER v. HARRIS

401 U.S. 37(1971).

NATURE OF CASE: Appeal from an injunction against a pending state prosecution.

FACT SUMMARY: After being indicted in a California state court for violation of the California Criminal Syndicalism Act, Harris (P) filed suit in the federal district court seeking an injunction against Younger (D), the District Attorney, restraining him from further prosecution on the ground that the Act was overbroad and violated Harris' first and fourteenth amendment rights.

CONCISE RULE OF LAW: Federal courts should not interfere with pending state court proceedings except where it can be shown that the defendant will suffer irreparable injury.

FACTS: Harris (P) was indicted in a state court for violation of the California Criminal Syndicalism Act. Harris (P) then filed a complaint in the federal district court seeking an injunction against Younger (D), the District Attorney in charge of the state prosecution, restraining him from prosecuting Harris (P) further. Harris (P) alleged that the prosecution and even the presence of the Act violated his first and fourteenth amendment rights. A three-judge district court held that the act was void for vagueness and overbreadth in violation of the first and fourteenth amendments and granted the injunction. Younger (D) appealed on the ground that national policy forbids federal courts from enjoining pending state proceedings.

ISSUE: Can federal courts stay or enjoin pending state court proceedings absent special circumstances showing irreparable injury?

HOLDING AND DECISION: (Black, J.) No. There is a national policy forbidding federal courts from staying or enjoining pending state court proceedings except under special circumstances where a person about to be prosecuted in a state court can show that he will suffer irreparable injury. In the instant case a proceeding was already pending in the state court, affording Harris an opportunity to raise his constitutional claims. Furthermore, there is no suggestion that this single prosecution against Harris is brought in bad faith or is meant to be one of a series of repeated prosecutions designed to harass him. The existence of a chilling effect, even in the area of first amendment rights, has never been considered a sufficient basis, in and of itself, for prohibiting state action. In the first place, the chilling effect cannot be satisfactorily eliminated by federal injunctive relief. Secondly, where a statute does not directly abridge free speech, but tends to have an incidental effect, it is well established that the statute can be upheld if the effect is minor in relation to the need for control of the conduct. Therefore, this court holds that the possible unconstitutionality of a statute on its face does not in itself justify an injunction against good-faith attempts to enforce it. Harris has failed to make any showing of bad faith, harassment, or any other unusual circumstance that would result in irreparable injury and call for equitable relief.

CONCURRENCE: (Brennan, J.) Harris was indicted in state court before he sued in federal court and his constitutional contentions may be adequately adjudicated in the state criminal proceeding.

CONCURRENCE: (Stewart, J.) Since this case and the others considered in the decision all involve state criminal prosecutions, the court does not deal with the factors that should govern a federal court when it is asked to intervene in state civil proceedings. The balance in such cases might be struck differently.

DISSENT: (Douglas, J.) The Younger case should fall within the scope of Dombrowski v. Pfister. That case represents an exception to the general rule that federal courts should not interfere with state criminal prosecutions. The exception does not arise merely because prosecutions are threatened to which the first amendment will be the proffered defense. Dombrowski governs statutes that have an overbroad sweep. The special circumstances when federal intervention in a state criminal proceeding is permissible are not restricted to bad faith on the part of state officials or the threat of multiple prosecutions. They also exist where for any reason the state statute being enforced is unconstitutional on its face. In Younger criminal syndicalism is defined so broadly as to jeopardize teaching that socialism is preferable to free enterprise. In Younger there is a prosecution under an unconstitutional statute and relief is denied. A federal injunction should issue under § 1983.

EDITOR'S ANALYSIS: In state criminal prosecutions unrelated to freedom of expression defendants have been unable to attain Dombrowski type relief. However, in cases where state action has been found to have a chilling effect on first amendment rights lower courts have granted Dombrowski sanctioned relief in a wide range of cases. These cases have usually involved prosecutions against civil rights workers or protest demonstrators under statutes unconstitutional on their face or under statutes applied in an unconstitutional manner.

NOTES:

SAMUELS v. MACKELL

401 U.S. 66 (1971).

NATURE OF CASE: Actions seeking injuncture and declaratory relief.

FACT SUMMARY: Samuels (P), indicted for allegedly violating the New York criminal anarchy statute, sued Mackell (D), claiming that the statute was unconstitutional and invalid.

CONCISE RULE OF LAW: Once a state criminal prosecution has commenced, a federal court should not issue a declaratory judgment in the case unless, under the circumstances, injunctive relief would be appropriate.

FACTS: Samuels (P) and others (P) were indicted on charges of violating the New York state criminal anarchy statute. Prior to their state court trials, Samuels (P) and the others (P) filed actions in federal court against Mackell (D). Each action claimed that the anarchy statute was void for vagueness and violated the first and fourteenth amendments, that the statute had been preempted by federal law, and that the New York laws pertaining to the drawing of grand juries were unconstitutional. Samuels (P) et al. argued that their indictments would harass them and cause irreparable damage. Therefore, their actions prayed for either injunctive or declaratory relief. A three-judge panel dismissed the federal court actions, but Samuels (P) and the others (P) appealed.

ISSUE: Should a federal court grant declaratory relief during the pendency of a state criminal prosecution?

HOLDING AND DECISION: (Black, J.) No. Once a state criminal prosecution has commenced, a federal court should not issue a declaratory judgment in the case unless, under the circumstances, injunctive relief would be appropriate. A pending state court prosecution should be enjoined by a federal tribunal only where necessary to prevent irreparable injury. And, according to Great Lakes Dredge & Dock Co. v. Huffman, declaratory relief should be granted only under that same circumstance. Principles of federalism militate against federal court interference with pending state court actions. Since Samuels (P) and the others (P) have not demonstrated that their indictments will cause them irreparable injury, their federal actions for injunctive and declaratory relief were properly dismissed.

CONCURRENCE: (Douglas, J.) No federal intervention is appropriate since the state courts can effectively preserve the rights of those indicted.

CONCURRENCE: (Brennan, J.) Since there has been no showing of bad-faith harassment on the part of the state, neither a declaratory judgment nor an injunction is necessary.

EDITOR'S ANALYSIS: The Constitution establishes a system of federal courts, but also limits their jurisdiction. Crucial to the federal scheme is the notion that the state courts must be autonomous, i.e., free to operate without interference by the federal courts. Congress has reinforced the constitutional blueprint by enacting statutes which limit the power of federal courts to meddle in the affairs of their state counterparts. And, of course, cases such as Samuels v. Mackell and Younger v. Harris have further affirmed the proposition that state courts are to be protected from federal intervention.

NOTES:

STEFFEL v. THOMPSON

415 U.S. 452 (1974).

NATURE OF CASE: Appeal from an action seeking an injunction and declaratory relief.

FACT SUMMARY: Steffel (P), twice threatened with arrest if he did not stop distributing handbills protesting the Vietnam War on the exterior sidewalk of a shopping center, brought this action In a federal district court seeking an Injunction and a declaratory judgment that the applicable Georgia criminal trespass law was being applied in derogation of his first and fourteenth amendment rights.

CONCISE RULE OF LAW: Under the Declaratory Judgment Act, declaratory relief is intended to act as an alternative to injunctions and to be utilized to test the constitutionality of state criminal statutes in cases where injunctive relief would be unavailable.

FACTS: Steffel (P) was twice threatened with arrest if he did not stop distributing handbills protesting the Vietnam War on the sidewalk of a shopping center. Steffel (P) brought this action seeking a declaratory judgment that the Georgia criminal trespass law was being applied in violation of his first and fourteenth amendment rights, and an injunction restraining Thompson (D) and others from enforcing the state statute. The district court denied all relief and dismissed the action. Steffel (P) appealed only from the denial of declaratory relief. The court of appeals affirmed the lower court's judgment refusing declaratory relief, and stating that since declaratory relief would normally disrupt the state criminal justice system in the manner of injunctive relief, it follows that the same test of bad faith harassment is a prerequisite for declaratory relief. A petition for rehearing was denied and Steffel (P) appealed to the Supreme Court.

ISSUE: Can declaratory relief act as an alternative to injunction and be utilized to test the constitutionality of state criminal statutes in cases where injunctive relief would be unavailable?

HOLDING AND DECISION: (Brennan, J.) Yes. Although it is true that federal courts should ordinarily refrain from enjoining ongoing state criminal prosecutions, where no state proceeding is pending the propriety of granting federal declaratory relief may properly be considered independently of a request for injunctive relief. In the case at bar, the court of appeals held that because injunctive relief would not be appropriate since Steffel failed to demonstrate irreparable injury it followed that declaratory relief was also inappropriate. The court erred in treating the two requests as a single issue. Declaratory relief is expressly authorized to be used because it is a less harsh and abrasive remedy than the injunction. Furthermore, when no state criminal proceeding is pending at the time the federal complaint is filed, federal intervention does not result in duplicative legal proceedings, nor can it be interpreted as infringing upon the state court's ability to enforce constitutional principles. Declaratory relief does not necessarily bar prosecutions under a state statute, as a broad injunction would. A state prosecutor, after the federal court decision, may still bring a prosecution under the state statute, if he reasonably believes that the defendant's conduct is not constitutionally protected. What is clear, however, is that even though a declaratory judgment has the force and effect of a final judgment, it is a much milder form of relief than an injunction. Though it may be persuasive , it is not ultimately coercive; noncompliance with it may be inappropriate, but is not contempt. This court therefore holds that, regardless of whether injunctive relief may be appropriate , federal declaratory relief is not precluded when no state prosecution is pending and a federal plaintiff demonstrates, as Steffel (P) has done, a genuine threat of enforcement of a disputed state criminal statute. The judgment of the court of appeals is reversed and the case remanded.

CONCURRENCE: (Stewart, J.) Our decision today must not be understood as authorizing the invocation of federal declaratory judgment jurisdiction by a person who thinks a state criminal statute is unconstitutional, unless he can demonstrate a genuine threat of enforcement of the disputed statute. Cases where such a genuine threat can be demonstrated are exceedingly rare.

CONCURRENCE: (Rehnquist, J.) Any arrest prior to resolution of the federal action would constitute a pending prosecution and bar declaratory relief.

EDITOR'S ANALYSIS: In the two landmark cases in this area, Younger v. Harris and Samuels v. Mackell, the Supreme Court recognized that both injunctive and declaratory relief is precluded in situations where state prosecutions were pending when the federal action commenced. The Court was of the view that the Younger case made it clear that the necessary prerequisite of irreparable injury must be measured by bad faith harassment. This test must be applied to a request for injunctive relief against threatened state court criminal prosecution as well as against a pending prosecution. In Samuels the court carried its reasoning one step further by holding that the same test of bad faith harassment is necessary in a declaratory relief action.

NOTES:

HICKS v. MIRANDA

422 U.S. 332 (1975).

NATURE OF CASE: Action to declare a state obscenity statute unconstitutional and enjoin its enforcement.

FACT SUMMARY: After Miranda (D) filed a federal action to declare California's obscenity statute unconstitutional and enjoin its enforcement, a criminal charge based on it was filed against him.

CONCISE RULE OF LAW: The rule that federal declaratory or injunctive relief is generally precluded if a state criminal charge is pending encompasses the situation where the state criminal charge is filed any time subsequent to commencement of the federal action but "before any proceedings of substance on the merits have taken place in the federal court."

FACTS: Miranda (D), whose employees were subjected to an eight-count misdemeanor charge for being involved with the showing of the motion picture "Deep Throat" at his theatres, sought federal declaratory and injunctive relief. Before the necessary three-judge federal panel was convened to determine the constitutionality of the California obscenity statute, District Attorney Hicks (P) amended the criminal complaint to include Miranda (D). Thereafter, the federal panel found the statute unconstitutional. The court rejected Hicks' (P) contention that Younger v. Harris' (401 U.S. 37 [1971]) general rule precluding federal interference with pending state prosecutions applied. The court also held no state prosecution had been pending when the federal action was filed, so the federal action was not precluded.

ISSUE: In general, is federal declaratory or injunctive relief precluded when a state criminal charge is filed after the federal action is filed but before any proceedings of substance on the merits?

HOLDING AND DECISION: (White, J.) Yes. The general rule expressed in Younger v. Harris is that federal declaratory or injunctive relief is precluded if a state criminal charge is pending. This rule applies to situations where, as here, the state criminal charge is filed any time subsequent to commencement of the federal action but "before any proceedings of substance on the merits have taken place in the federal court." Thus, this complaint should have been dismissed. Reversed.

DISSENT: (Stewart, J.) This decision is an open invitation to state officials to institute state proceedings in order to defeat federal jurisdiction. It also offends principles of federalism by ousting the federal courts from their historic role as the "primary reliances" for vindicating constitutional freedoms.

EDITOR'S ANALYSIS: In a case decided one week later, the court upheld issuance of a temporary federal injunction while a federal action for declaratory relief against an anti-topless dancing ordinance was pending. Since those who brought the action had put tops on their dancers once the ordinance was passed, Hicks could not come into play because they did not remove their tops until the federal injunction issued and "proceedings of substance on the merits" had taken place in the federal court. Doran v. Salem Inn, Inc., 422 U.S. 922 (1975).

NOTES:

PENNZOIL CO. v. TEXACO INC.

107 S.Ct. 1519, 95 L.Ed. 1 (1987).

NATURE OF CASE: Appeal from affirmation of grant of injunctive relief.

FACT SUMMARY: Pennzoil (D) appealed from the affirmation of the district court's decision granting Texaco (P) injunctive relief, contending the court should have abstained from interfering in the execution of Pennzoil's (D) judgment against Texaco (P) in state court.

CONCISE RULE OF LAW: In actions seeking injunctive relief from the execution of a state court judgment pending appeal in the state courts, federal courts should abstain if the grant of relief would constitute a significant intrusion on the state's judicial system.

FACTS: Pennzoil (D) obtained a state court verdict against Texaco (P) for $11 billion. Pennzoil (D) obtained significant rights under state law against Texaco (P). The bond to suspend the judgment under state law would have been $13 billion. Even prior to the entry of judgment, the financial effect of the burden was severe. Prior to the entry of judgment, Texaco (P) filed an action for injunctive relief in federal court. Texaco (P) had not argued in the state courts that execution of the judgment conflicted with federal law. The district court granted relief, and the court of appeals affirmed, finding that it had jurisdiction over Texaco's (P) constitutional claims, that Texaco (P) had stated a claim under 42 U.S.C. § 1983, that abstention was not required, and that the merits favored Texaco (P). From this decision, Pennzoil (D) appealed.

ISSUE: In actions seeking injunctive relief from the execution of a state court judgment pending appeal in the state courts, should federal courts abstain if the grant of relief would constitute a significant intrusion on the state's judicial system?

HOLDING AND DECISION: (Powell, J.) Yes. In actions seeking injunctive relief from the execution of a state court judgment pending appeal in the state courts, federal courts should abstain if the grant of relief would constitute a significant intrusion on the state's judicial system. Significant state interests are harmed in this situation absent abstention. An important, underlying reason for the abstention doctrine is the notion of comity, a proper respect for state functions. Abstention is appropriate where the exercise of judicial power disregards this comity. Abstention also avoids the unwarranted determination of constitutional questions. Decisions in this situation are unwarranted and nonbinding on state courts. Texaco (P) did not raise these constitutional questions in the state courts, and federal courts should assume that the state courts afford an adequate remedy, absent unambiguous authority to the contrary. Finally, the evidence is clear that the state courts had the power to entertain constitutional challenges to its enforcement provisions. The district court should have abstained. Reversed.

CONCURRENCE: (Brennan, J.) Abstention is in general inapplicable to civil proceedings. The court erred in not addressing the merits of the case.

CONCURRENCE: (Blackmun, J.) This case presents an example of the "narrowly limited special circumstances," where issues of state law are still clouded and which warrants abstention.

EDITOR'S ANALYSIS: The complexity and enormity of the issues presented led to the proliferation of differing rationales in the current case. Those Justices who would have reached the merits appear to be in agreement that Texaco's (P) claims were without merit. The decision in this case no doubt contributed to Texaco's (P) entering Ch. 11 rehabilitation six days following the decision.

NOTES:

NOTES

CHAPTER 17
HABEAS CORPUS

QUICK REFERENCE RULES OF LAW

1. **Dismissal.** A federal court must dismiss a habeas corpus petition containing any claims that have not been exhausted in state court. (Rose v. Lundy)

2. **Prisoners.** A prisoner is not entitled to federal habeas corpus relief for unconstitutionally obtained evidence introduced at trial if the state has provided an opportunity to fully and fairly litigate the claim. (Stone v. Powell)

3. **Retroactive Application of Rules.** New rules should be applied retroactively to cases on collateral review only when the rules place private acts beyond criminal lawmaking authority or when they implicate fundamental fairness of the trial. (Teague v. Lane)

4. **Noncompliance with a State Contemporaneous Objection Rule.** Federal habeas corpus will not be available to a defendant whose appeal is not granted due to noncompliance with a state contemporaneous objection rule, unless the defendant had good cause not to object. (Wainright v. Sykes)

NOTES

WAINWRIGHT v. SYKES

433 U.S. 72 (1977).

NATURE OF CASE: Appeal in a habeas corpus proceeding.

FACT SUMMARY: Sykes (D) sought habeas corpus when state appellate courts refused to consider his conviction appeal because the basis for the appeal was not raised at trial.

CONCISE RULE OF LAW: Federal habeas corpus will not be available to a defendant whose appeal is not granted due to noncompliance with a state contemporaneous objection rule, unless the defendant had good cause not to object.

FACTS: Sykes (D) was arrested for homicide. He was given his Miranda warning. He then indicated a wish to speak and confessed. At trial, the confession was entered into evidence. No objection was made, and he was convicted. On appeal, he argued that the confession was not voluntary. The state appellate court refused to consider the appeal, holding that Sykes (D) had not objected at trial, a necessity for review under state procedural rules. Sykes (D) petitioned for habeas corpus. A district court ordered the state appellate court to hold a voluntariness hearing. The Fifth Circuit affirmed. The Supreme Court granted review.

ISSUE: Will federal habeas corpus be available to a defendant whose appeal is not granted due to noncompliance with a state contemporaneous objection rule, if the defendant did not have good cause not to object?

HOLDING AND DECISION: (Rehnquist, J.) No. Federal habeas corpus will not be available to a defendant whose appeal is not granted due to noncompliance with a state contemporaneous objection rule, unless the defendant had good cause not to object. It has long been an issue in the federal judiciary as to the extent to which independent state grounds will bar otherwise available federal habeas review. It has been established that a state decision based on substantive law will not be reviewed. A similar rule once held sway respecting procedural rules, but this authority has been overruled. Nonetheless, good reasons exist for accepting the procedural bar in this instance. First, it has been already held that the Constitution does not require a voluntariness hearing absent a contemporaneous challenge. The contemporaneous challenge rule is widespread and this militates in favor of federal respect for it. Contemporaneous objections are to be encouraged. First, an exclusion may be granted at trial, making a petition for habeas corpus unnecessary. Also, not to enforce the rule would encourage "sandbagging" by defense counsel, who might take their chances on a not guilty verdict without objecting, knowing they can raise the objection later. Finally, to the greatest extent possible, trials are to be the major vehicle for determinations of guilt and innocence. Policy dictates that as much be litigated there as possible. For these reasons, only if a defendant has good cause for not objecting at trial may he petition for habeas corpus review in the face of a contemporaneous objection rule not followed. Here, Sykes (D) has shown no good cause. Reversed.

CONCURRENCE: (Burger, C.J.) The standard adopted by the lower courts, that a defendant had to deliberately choose not to object to be precluded from review, was entirely without foundation.

CONCURRENCE: (Stevens, J.) The court was wise not to attempt to define the scope of "cause" for not objecting. Many factors enter into this analysis.

CONCURRENCE: (White, J.) The deliberate choice rule should be followed, but the burden should be placed on the petitioning defendant to disprove deliberate choice.

DISSENT: (Brennan, J.) The deliberate choice, or "deliberate bypasss" rule, best accommodates the rights of a defendant and proper respect for the integrity of state judicial systems. The "cause" rule enunciated here provides no guidance whatsoever for lower courts. Finally, left unanswered is the important question of how to treat an objection not raised due to incompetent counsel.

EDITOR'S ANALYSIS: The "deliberate bypass" rule was first announced in Fay v. Noia, 372 U.S. 391 (1963). It did not hold a prominent place for long. The more deferential "cause" test was enunciated in Davis v. United States, 411 U.S. 233 (1973), and was given broader application by the present action.

NOTES:

STONE v. POWELL
428 U.S. 465 (1976).

NATURE OF CASE: Review of grant of habeas corpus relief.

FACT SUMMARY: Powell (P) petitioned for federal habeas corpus relief on the grounds that evidence obtained in an unconstitutional search or seizure was introduced at his murder trial.

CONCISE RULE OF LAW: A prisoner is not entitled to federal habeas corpus relief for unconstitutionally obtained evidence introduced at trial if the state has provided an opportunity to fully and fairly litigate the claim.

FACTS: Powell (P) was involved in a dispute with a liquor store manager in California. A fight broke out, and the store manager was shot. Powell (P) was arrested ten hours later in Nevada for violation of a vagrancy law. In the search incident to arrest, a gun matching the type used in the murder was found. Powell (P) was extradited and convicted of the murder. Powell (P) argued at trial that the officer's testimony and the revolver should have been excluded because the vagrancy ordinance was unconstitutional, and thus the search was illegal. The trial court rejected this claim, and the court of appeals affirmed. Powell's federal writ of habeas corpus was denied in district court. The court of appeals, however, reversed. Stone (D) petitioned for certiorari.

ISSUE: Is a prisoner entitled to federal habeas corpus relief for unconstitutionally obtained evidence introduced at trial if the state has provided an opportunity to fully and fairly litigate the claim?

HOLDING AND DECISION: (Powell, J.) No. A prisoner is not entitled to federal habeas corpus relief for unconstitutionally obtained evidence introduced at trial if the state has provided an opportunity to fully and fairly litigate the claim. The exclusionary rule keeps reliable evidence out of the courts as a deterrent to police officers. Often the error is minimal compared to the guilt of the defendant. However, the collateral review of the exclusionary rules involved here is so far removed from the activity of the law enforcement officers that it cannot be understood to further any deterrent effect. Reversed.

DISSENT: (Brennan, J.) State court must exclude evidence obtained in violation of the Fourth Amendment. The court changes the Fourth Amendment from a personal right (applied to each individual) into a general enforcement of procedure for the rights.

EDITOR'S ANALYSIS: The thrust of the majority's opinion is that collateral review may allow a guilty person to go free. The Court concludes that the state court's finding of guilt, no matter how obtained, precludes an assumption of innocence until proven guilty. This thinking contradicts the rationale of the Fourth Amendment.

NOTES:

TEAGUE v. LANE

489 U.S. 288 (1989).

NATURE OF CASE: Appeal from denial of habeas corpus relief.

NOTES:

FACT SUMMARY: Teague (P), a black man, was convicted by an all-white petit jury and contended that a Supreme Court decision prohibiting exclusion of a juror by race should be retroactively applied to him.

CONCISE RULE OF LAW: New rules should be applied retroactively to cases on collateral review only when the rules place private acts beyond criminal lawmaking authority or when they implicate fundamental fairness of the trial.

FACTS: The prosecutors at Teagues's (P) criminal trial used all ten of their preemptory challenges to exclude blacks from the jury. Teague (P), a black man, twice moved for a mistrial and was denied. He was convicted by an all-white jury. The conviction was upheld on direct review. Teague (P) filed a writ of habeas corpus claiming he was deprived of a fair cross-section of the population on his jury as required under later caselaw. His writ was denied by both the district court and the court of appeals. The Supreme Court granted certiorari.

ISSUE: Should new rules be applied retroactively to cases on collateral review only when they place private acts beyond criminal lawmaking authority or when they implicate fundamental fairness of the trial?

HOLDING AND DECISION: (O'Connor, J.) Yes. New rules should be applied retroactively to cases on collateral review only when the rules place private acts beyond criminal lawmaking authority or when they implicate the fundamental fairness of the trial. Applying the fair cross-section rule to petit juries would be a new rule and thus must fit into one of the above exceptions in order to apply retroactively to Teauge's (P) case. The first exception involving private acts does not apply to this case. Neither does the second. The fact that Teague (P) was not tried by a racially integrated jury does not implicate the fairness of his trial and thus does not meet the standard required for the second exception. The court of appeals is affirmed.

CONCURRENCE: (White, J.) If we are wrong in determining the breadth of collateral review it is Congress' s job to correct us.

CONCURRENCE: (Stevens, J.) The court should first determine whether there is a violation of a constitutional rule before proceeding to determine that the error does not apply retroactively.

DISSENT: (Brennan, J.) The majority curtails the reach of the writ of habeas corpus without reference to stare decisis solely to ensure that all defendants are treated alike.

EDITOR'S ANALYSIS: The Teague holding may aid a defendant in cases where a defendant relies on a constitutional ruling at trial and the ruling is later overruled. However, the rule is fundamentally designed to ensure finality and closure — attributes that typically work to the benefit of the state. Cases following Teague have mainly turned on the issue of whether the case at hand was controlled by a prior ruling or by a "new rule."

ROSE v. LUNDY
455 U.S. 509 (1982).

NATURE OF CASE: Review of grant of petition for writ of habeas corpus.

FACT SUMMARY: Lundy (P) was convicted of rape in state court but successfully proved that he did not receive a fair trial in a subsequent habeas corpus proceeding.

CONCISE RULE OF LAW: A federal court must dismiss a habeas corpus petition containing any claims that have not been exhausted in state court.

FACTS: Lundy (P) was convicted of rape and sentenced to a state prison term. The state court of appeals affirmed the conviction, and the state supreme court denied review. Lundy (D) then petitioned for a writ of habeas corpus based on four claims, two of which had not been exhausted in the state courts. The district court, although acknowledging that it was improper to consider the unexhausted claims, found that Lundy (P) did not recceive a fair trial upon those claims. The court of appeals affirmed. Rose (D), the warden of the prison where Lundy (P) was being held petitioned for review, which the Supreme Court granted.

ISSUE: Must a federal court dismiss a habeas corpus petition containing claims that have not been exhausted in state court?

HOLDING AND DECISION: (O'Connor, J.) Yes. A federal court must dismiss a habeas corpus petition containing claims that have not been exhausted in state court. The habeas statute requires a prisoner to exhaust all state remedies before turning to the federal courts. This "total exhaustion" requirement prevents courts from having to determine if the exhausted claims are dependent on the unexhausted claims. Total exhaustion is simple, straightforward, and will avoid piecemeal litigation. This holding does not prohibit Lundy (P) from refiling the writ citing only unexhausted claims and thus does not interfere with Lundy's (P) right to speedy relief. Reversed

CONCURRENCE: (Blackmun, J.) This case should be remanded with directions to the district court to dismiss the unexhausted claims and then to determine if the exhausted claim merited collateral relief.

DISSENT: (Brennan, J.) Total exhaustion is a protection against abuse of the writ but should only be applied to those who intentionally withhold claims in an attempt get two hearings.

EDITOR'S ANALYSIS: In McClesky v. Zant, 499 U.S. 467 (1991), the court placed the initial burden of showing abuse of writ on the government. However, it also ruled that once the government has set out the writ history and the allegation of abuse, the petitioner must justify his failure to bring all claims at once. Even if he cannot show cause, the failure to raise a claim may be excused anyway if he can show that a fundamental miscarriage of justice would otherwise result.

NOTES:

CHAPTER 18
CIVIL RIGHTS REMOVAL

QUICK REFERENCE RULES OF LAW

1. **Claims under the Fourteenth Amendment.** The removal of claims under the Fourteenth Amendment applies only to those violations that arise before trial. (Virginia v. Rives)

2. **Racial Equality and Removal to Federal Court.** A state court defendant is entitled to removal to federal court if his case involves the assertion of a right that arises under a law providing for racial equality, and there is a legitimate basis for predicting that he will be denied or prevented from enjoying that right in a state court. (Georgia v. Rachel)

3. **Section 1443.** Section 1443, which authorizes removal of a civil action or criminal prosecution for any act under color of authority derived from any law providing for equal rights, is available only to federal officers and persons assisting such officers in the performance of their official duties. (City of Greenwood v. Peacock)

NOTES

VIRGINIA v. RIVES

100 U.S. (10 Otto) 313 (1879).

NATURE OF CASE: Petition for habeas corpus following denial of removal of a criminal case.

FACT SUMMARY: Burwell and Lee Reynolds (P), two black criminal defendants, were convicted by an all-white jury for the murder of a white man after their request for removal to federal court was denied.

CONCISE RULE OF LAW: The removal of claims under the Fourteenth Amendment applies only to those violations that arise before trial.

FACTS: Burwell and Lee Reynolds (P) were indicted for the murder of a white man. At trial, they filed a motion to have the all-white jury pool recomposed to include one-third black men. This motion was denied on the ground that the pool was compiled according to law. They then moved for removal to federal court based on the fact that they were being denied equal protection of the laws under the Fourteenth Amendment. This motion was also denied, and the defendants were tried separately and convicted. They then filed for habeas corpus relief.

ISSUE: Does the removal of claims under the Fourteenth Amendment apply only to those violations that arise before trial?

HOLDING AND DECISION: (Strong, J.) Yes. The removal of claims under the Fourteenth Amendment applies only to those violations that arise before trial. Under the removal statute, in cases where a citizen cannot protect or enforce any civil rights granted to citizens of the United States, the party can petition for removal. But the remedy of removal is only available where the violation is a function of state law and thus raises the inability to enforce equal civil rights. In order to qualify for removal, the state statute has to reference the unequal treatment; this statute, which merely describes the requirements of potential jurors, does not. The motion for removal was correctly denied.

EDITOR'S ANALYSIS: In Strauder v. West Virginia, 100 U.S. (10 Otto) 303 (1879), the Court on similar facts ruled that removal was allowed because the state statute allowed only white men to serve as jurors. In Rives, the Virginia statue nominally allowed blacks to serve (or at least did not exclude them), although the evidence at trial showed no blacks had ever done so.

NOTES:

GEORGIA v. RACHEL

384 U.S. 780 (1966).

NATURE OF CASE: Petition for removal of state criminal trespass prosecutions.

FACT SUMMARY: Rachel (D) and others (D) were arrested for criminal trespass when they attempted to obtain service at Georgia (P) restaurants known to discriminate against Negroes.

CONCISE RULE OF LAW: A state court defendant is entitled to removal to federal court if his case involves the assertion of a right that arises under a law providing for racial equality, and there is a legitimate basis for predicting that he will be denied or prevented from enjoying that right in a state court.

FACTS: Rachel (D) and nineteen others (D) were arrested and charged with criminal trespass when, at various times during the spring of 1963, they attempted to obtain service at certain Atlanta restaurants that were open to the public. Rachel (D) and the others (D) were scheduled for trials in a Georgia (P) court, but they petitioned for removal of their ceses to federal district court. They alleged that their arrests had occurred because of a desire to perpetuate the racially discriminatory policies and practices that had long prevented Negroes from eating at the restaurants involved. Indictments then followed pursuant to a Georgia statute which made it a misdemeanor to refuse to leave another's premises after having been requested by the owner to do so. The petition for removal was based on 28 USC § 1443 and charged that the arrestees (D) were being denied or were unable to enforce rights arising under the Constitution or laws of the United States relating to the equal rights of citizens. On its own motion without a hearing, the federal district court remanded the cases to the Georgia (P) courts, holding that removal was inappropriate. The court of appeals reversed, however, and the Supreme Court eventually granted certiorari to determine whether the petition presented facts warranting removal.

ISSUE: May his case be removed to federal court if a state court criminal defendant demonstrates that he will otherwise be prevented from enjoying his right to racial equality?

HOLDING AND DECISION: (Stewart, J.) Yes. A state court defendant is entitled to removal to federal court if his case involves the assertion of a right that arises under a law providing for racial equality and there is a legitimate basis for predicting that he will be denied or prevented from enforcing that right in a state court. Since the district court ordered the remand, Congress has passed the Civil Rights Act of 1964. And in Hamm v. City of Rock Hill, 379 U.S. 306, 311(1964), this court held that the Act precluded state trespass prosecutions based on peaceful attempts to be served in establishments covered by the Act, even if those prosecutions commenced prior to the effective date of the Act. Section 1443, the statute upon which the petition for removal is based, has been construed by a long line of cases. The rule that has evolved dictates that where the claimed right to racial equality derives from a statute such as the Civil Rights Act, removal is appropriate if that right is unlikely to be vindicated in the state court. It has also been established that pretrial removal should take place only when a statute is the basis for the state court's denial of or refusal to enforce the right to racial equality. In this case, the Georgia (P) statute pursuant to which the indictments occurred is the basis for the alleged denial of that right. Thus, Rachel (D) and the others (D) could not be prosecuted, much less convicted and sentenced, by any Georgia (P) court. It follows that the judgment reversing the remand to the state court must be affirmed.

DISSENT: (Douglas, J.) The right to receive nondiscriminatory service in restaurants is at stake here. If Rachel (D) and the others (D) were ejected for racially motivated reasons, their prosecutions should be dismissed. If they were ousted for some other reason, removal is not appropriate, and the state courts may continue their pending prosecutions. The presence or absence of a racial motive may be established at the hearing of the petition for removal.

EDITOR'S ANALYSIS: The ALI expresses a preference for injunctive relief rather than removal in cases involving facts similar or analogous to those of Georgia v. Rachel. Some commentators agree that the enjoining of state proceedings is a less drastic remedy and reflects less unfavorably upon the state court. However, other text writers reason that an injunction is no less offensive to state court judges than removal would be, and that it is at least as easy and efficient to decide on removal, rather than pursuant to a suit seeking an injunction, whether or not a state court will adequately protect a defendant's right to equality.

NOTES:

CITY OF GREENWOOD v. PEACOCK

384 U.S. 808 (1966).

NATURE OF CASE: Appeal from prosecution of various criminal charges.

FACT SUMMARY: Several consolidated cases involved prosecutions on various state criminal charges against twenty-nine people allegedly engaged in civil rights activities in Leflore County, Mississippi.

CONCISE RULE OF LAW: Section 1443, which authorizes removal of a civil action or criminal prosecution for any act under color of authority derived from any law providing for equal rights, is available only to federal officers and persons assisting such officers in the performance of their official duties.

FACTS: Several consolidated cases involved prosecutions on various state criminal charges against twenty-nine people allegedly engaged in civil rights activities in Leflore County, Mississippi. In the first case, fourteen individuals were charged with obstructing the public streets of the City of Greenwood (P) in violation of Mississippi law. Peacock (D) and others (D) filed petitions to remove their cases to the U.S. District Court under Section 1443. Alleging that they were members of a civil rights group engaged in a drive to encourage black voter registration, their petitions stated that (1) they were denied or could not enforce in the state courts rights under laws providing for the civil rights of U.S. citizens and (2) they were prosecuted for acts committed under color of authority of the Constitution. Additionally, Peacock (D) alleged that the statute under which they were charged was unconstitutionally vague on its face and part of a policy of racial discrimination. The district court sustained the motion of Greenwood (P) to remand the cases to the city police court for trial. The court of appeals reversed. Greenwood (P) appealed to the Supreme Court.

ISSUE: Is Section 1443, which authorizes removal of a civil action or criminal prosecution for any act under color of authority derived from any law providing for equal rights, available only to federal officers and persons assisting such officers in the performance of their official duties?

HOLDING AND DECISION: (Stewart, J.) Yes. Section 1443, which authorizes removal of a civil action or criminal prosecution for any act under color of authority derived from any law providing for equal rights, is available only to federal officers and persons assisting such officers in the performance of their official duties. Accordingly, Peacock (D) and the other petitioners had no right of removal to federal court under Section 1443(2). To sustain removal of these prosecutions to federal court upon the allegations of the petitions would mark a complete departure from the terms of the removal statute, which allows removal only when a person is denied or cannot enforce a specified federal right in the state courts. Under § 1443(1), the vindication of the defendant's federal rights is left to the state courts except in rare situations where it can be clearly predicted by reason of the operation of a pervasive and explicit state or federal law that those rights will inevitably be denied by the very act of bringing the defendant to trial in the state court. If, in fact, the petitioners in the present case are being prosecuted on baseless charges solely because of their race, their most obvious remedy is vindication of their federal claims on direct review in this court, not removal to a federal district court. Therefore, the judgment of the court of appeals is reversed.

DISSENT: (Douglas, J.) If the federal court is persuaded that the state court indeed will not make a good-faith effort to apply the paramount federal law pertaining to equal civil rights, then the federal court must accept the removal and try the case on the merits. The result of removal is not the transfer of the trial from the state to federal courts. If, after hearing, it does not appear that the state prosecution is being used to deny federal rights, the case is remanded for trial in the state courts. But the removal statute meanwhile serves a protective function.

EDITOR'S ANALYSIS: The court in the present case also addressed itself to the other remedies available in the federal courts to redress wrongs of the type claimed by the petitioners. For example, if the state prosecution or trial would itself clearly deny their rights protected by the First Amendment, they may, under some circumstances obtain an injunction in the federal courts. Also, if at their trial they are in fact denied any federal constitutional rights and these denials go uncorrected by other courts of the state, the remedy of federal habeas corpus is freely available to them.

NOTES:

NOTES

CHAPTER 19
RES JUDICATA IN THE FEDERAL SYSTEM

QUICK REFERENCE RULES OF LAW

1. **Unavailability of Federal Habeas Corpus Relief.** Unavailability of federal habeas corpus relief does not render the doctrine of collateral estoppel inapplicable to a § 1983 suit. (Allen v. McCurry)

2. **Res Judicata.** A federal claim that could have been raised in the state court proceeding but was not is precluded by res judicata. (Migra v. Warren City School District Board of Education)

3. **State Preclusion Law.** In deciding whether a state court judgment bars a subsequent federal lawsuit, a federal court must first consider state preclusion law. (Marrese v. American Academy of Orthopaedic Surgeons)

NOTES

ALLEN v. McCURRY

449 U.S. 90 (1980).

NATURE OF CASE: Appeal from reinstatement of action under § 1983 seeking $1 million in damages.

FACT SUMMARY: After McCurry (P) was arrested and convicted pursuant to an unconstitutional search and seizure, he filed a § 1983 action against Allen (D) and the other arresting officer (D).

CONCISE RULE OF LAW: Unavailability of federal habeas corpus relief does not render the doctrine of collateral estoppel inapplicable to a § 1983 suit.

FACTS: Allen (D) and another officer, Jacobsmeyer (D), received a tip that McCurry (P) was selling heroin. When they attempted to purchase some from him, he shot at them. The officers (D) then entered the house, searched it, found drugs, and arrested McCurry (P). At trial and on appeal, McCurry (P) raised the unlawful search and seizure defense, which was partially rejected. He was convicted and then denied a writ of habeas corpus because the court found that his constitutional claims had been fully and fairly litigated. The court of appeals reversed and remanded. Allen (D) and Jacobsmeyer (D) appealed, arguing that they should be permitted to raise the state court's rejection of McCurry's (P) constitutional claim as a collateral estoppel defense.

ISSUE: Does unavailability of federal habeas corpus render the doctrine of collateral estoppel inapplicable to a § 1983 action?

HOLDING AND DECISION: (Stewart, J.) No. Unavailability of federal habeas corpus relief does not render the doctrine of collateral estoppel inapplicable to a § 1983 suit. Section 1983 was intended to protect federal rights that the states were unable or unwilling to enforce. Thus, to the extent someone was unable to fully and fairly litigate these issues, the effects of collateral estoppel would be precluded. In this case McCurry (P) had the opportunity, and took it, to raise these issues in state court. He is now collaterally estopped form relitigating them. Thus, the state courts' findings on the exclusionary rule precluded McCurry's (P) suit under § 1983. The court of appeals is reversed.

DISSENT: (Blackmun, J.) A criminal defendant is not free to choose his forum, and the remedy for § 1983 versus the remedy for the exclusionary rule are so different as to merit particular consideration.

EDITOR'S ANALYSIS: The majority's holding does not take into consideration the difference between a civil and a criminal action. A defendant who raises federal issues at his trial is not doing so of free will but to avoid a later finding that he waived such rights. Justice Stevens would apply the factors of Montana v. United States, 440 U.S. 12467 (1979), to find special circumstances in criminal cases and thus warrant an exception to the rule of preclusion.

NOTES:

MIGRA v. WARREN CITY SCHOOL DISTRICT BOARD OF EDUCATION

465 U.S. 75 (1984).

NATURE OF CASE: Appeal from summary judgment for the defense in § 1983 claim of violation of First Amendment rights.

FACT SUMMARY: Migra's (P) annual employment as a school supervisor was renewed and then revoked by the Warren City School Board (D), prompting her to sue first in state court and then in federal court on the omitted § 1983 claims.

CONCISE RULE OF LAW: A federal claim that could have been raised in the state court proceeding but was not is precluded by res judicata.

FACTS: Migra (P) was employed on an annual basis by the Warren City School District (D). The School Board (D) voted to renew Migra's (P) employment, which she accepted. Six days later, however, the Board (D) passed a motion not to renew Migra's (P) employment. When Migra (P) was informed of this, she filed a state court action for breach of contract and conspiracy to interfere with contract. The trial court found for Migra (P) on the issue of breach of contract and dismissed the other claim without prejudice. The court of appeals affirmed. The state supreme court denied review. Migra (P) then filed a federal court action against the Board (D) for interfering with her First Amendment rights. She asserted that her activity on a board to investigate desegregation had prompted the Board's (D) action. The district court granted the motion for summary judgment based on res judicata and dismissed the case. The court of appeals affirmed. The Supreme Court granted certiorari.

ISSUE: Is a federal claim that could have been raised in the state court proceeding, but was not, precluded by res judicata?

HOLDING AND DECISION: (Blackmun, J.) A federal claim that could have been raised in the state court proceeding, but was not, is precluded by res judicata. Congress implemented § 1983 because of its distrust of the ability of state courts to protect federal rights, thus giving litigants a supplementary forum when state courts proved unreliable. However § 1983 did not open the way to relitigation of an issue already determined in a state proceeding, or of any issue, that could have been so determined. Migra (P) cannot proceed to judgment on her state claims and then turn to federal court for adjudication of her federal claims. It is more important to give full faith and credit to state-court judgments than to ensure separate forums, regardless of the relative expertise each court might bring to the issues. Therefore, Migra's (P) state-court judgment in this litigation has the same preclusive effect in federal court as it would have in an Ohio state court. The judgment of the court of appeals is vacated, and the case is remanded to district court so that it may apply Ohio state preclusion law.

CONCURRENCE: (White, J.) The federal courts should be free to apply the rules of res judicata and collateral estoppel that they have developed, even if such rules would have different results than their state counterparts.

EDITOR'S ANALYSIS: Note that the full faith and credit principles binding state and federal courts are not found in the Constitution; Article IV applies to judgments of sister states only. Rather, the principles are found in § 1738 of the United States Code. Federal full faith and credit obligation is subject to congressional modification or abandonment.

NOTES:

MARRESE v. AMERICAN ACADEMY OF ORTHOPEDIC SURGEONS

470 U.S. 373 (1985).

NATURE OF CASE: Review of dismissal of antitrust suit.

FACT SUMMARY: After Marrese (P) and Treister (P) sought relief in state court to gain membership in the American Academy of Orthopedic Surgeons (AAOS)(D), their federal antitrust claim was barred by res judicata.

CONCISE RULE OF LAW: In deciding whether a state court judgment bars a subsequent federal lawsuit, a federal court must first consider state preclusion law.

FACTS: Orthopaedic surgeons Marrese (P) and Treister (P) were denied membership in the AAOS (D). Neither was given a reason for the denial, nor were they given a hearing. Dr. Treister (P) and Dr. Marrese (P) each filed suits in state court claiming that the decision violated common law rights of association. Neither raised state antitrust claims. Their cases were ultimately dismissed for failure to state a cause of action. Marrese (P) and Treister (P) filed a federal antitrust action against the AAOS (D) in federal court based on the same facts. The AAOS's (D) motion to dismiss was denied by the district court. The court of appeals reversed and dismissed, concluding that claim preclusion barred the federal antitrust suit. The Supreme Court granted certiorari.

ISSUE: In deciding whether a state court judgment bars a subsequent federal lawsuit, must a federal court first consider state preclusion law?

HOLDING AND DECISION: (O'Connor, J.) Yes. In deciding whether a state court judgment bars a subsequent federal lawsuit, a federal court must first consider state preclusion law. In this case, the decisions below did not consider Illinois preclusion law in their discussion of the claim preclusion issue. The district court relied on federal law to conclude that the state judgments did not bar Treister's (P) and Marrese's (P) claims under the Sherman Act since federal antitrust claims are within the exclusive jurisdiction of the federal courts. But exclusive federal jurisdiction does not necessarily render the full faith and credit statute inapplicable. Instead, a court must look first to state preclusion law in determining the preclusive effects of a state court judgment. The court of appeals also erred by omitting any discussion of Illinois principles of claim preclusion from its decision dismissing the case. Instead, it created a special exception to the full faith and credit statute for federal antitrust claims, giving state court judgments greater preclusive effect in order to foster judicial economy. This was incorrect. Reversed and remanded.

CONCURRENCE: (Burger, C.J.) Since Illinois preclusion law is ambiguous, it would be consistent with the full faith and credit statute to formulate a federal rule to resolve this matter — for example, the rule might state that a party is precluded from asserting a claim that he had a full and fair opportunity to litigate in a prior action.

EDITOR'S ANALYSIS: The res judicata doctrine seeks to conserve the resources of the litigants and the state by preventing the relitigation of certain issues in a subsequent proceeding. It is supposed to protect defendants from repetitive lawsuits based on the same conduct and require plaintiffs to litigate their claims in an economical fashion. These were the goals the court of appeals was supposedly attempting to promote when it informed Marrese (P) and Treister (P) that they should have either filed concurrent state and federal actions or brought their state claims in federal court pendant to their Sherman Act claim.

NOTES:

NOTES

NOTES